Priestland's Progress
Gerald Priestland

Gerald Priestland was educated at Charterhouse, Oxford – and the BBC. He joined the Corporation in 1949 as a journalist, and retired in 1982 after thirty-three years service during which he was a foreign correspondent in India, the Middle East and the United States, a programme presenter on radio and television, and finally Religious Affairs correspondent. He now works as a freelance broadcaster and author. His books include works on violence, the ethics of journalism and three volumes of his religious talks *Yours Faithfully*. He was brought up a Public School Anglican, became an English Presbyterian and is now a Quaker. He would rather have been a musician, but lacks the talent.

GERALD PRIESTLAND

PRIESTLAND'S PROGRESS

ONE MAN'S SEARCH FOR CHRISTIANITY NOW

ARIEL BOOKS
BBC PUBLICATIONS

First published 1981
Reprinted 1981 (twice), 1982 (twice)
First Ariel edition 1983, reprinted 1986

Published by BBC Publications
A division of BBC Enterprises Ltd
35 Marylebone High Street, London W1M 4AA

Printed in England by Mackays of Chatham Ltd

Set in 10 on 12 Palatino

ISBN 0 563 20113 4

Contents

Introduction

In 1977 I took up the job of BBC Religious Affairs Correspondent (to the astonishment of my fellow journalists) because I felt that there, if anywhere, I might find the meaning of the experiences, pleasant and unpleasant, that had gone before in my life. But the deeper I got into the work, the less I realised I knew about the foundations of religion. I had no formal training in divinity and I had barely paused to ask myself what I really believed, let alone why. That there was a God I had no doubt, and I dared to call myself a Christian: after all, I could hardly be a Hindu or a Jew. But was I really a Christian at all? The project of writing this book, and the radio series on which it is based, have compelled me to put that to the test, and perhaps a good many of my readers and listeners at the same time.

When my producer Chris Rees and I first announced the project there was not a little misgiving. High churchmen feared we would be too low, low churchmen were afraid we would be too high, and both were suspicious that I might convert the operation into a vehicle for my own Quaker heresies. The more we insisted that everyone would get a fair hearing, the louder the warning came that Christianity would simply be shown up as divided and self-destructive. Chris and I urged that our aim was to identify the common ground between the churches, which we felt to be wider than commonly supposed. But who were we to presume to define the faith? Our answer was that we claimed to be no more than ourselves, professional broadcasters who called themselves Christians, on a pilgrimage and in need of all the help we could get on the way. If the job was worth doing it could only be done by fallible human beings, and we were prepared to make fools of ourselves rather than leave it undone. I said that I was prepared to go out in front and take any *odium theologicum* that might be thrown at me.

To set us on our course we invited a panel of four eminent

advisers. It consisted of Bishop Stephen Neill of the Church of England, Bishop David Konstant of the Roman Catholic Church, the Reverend Doctor Gordon Rupp of the Methodists and Professor William Shaw of the Church of Scotland. Their main function was to help us identify a dozen key areas of the faith to which we might devote one programme each, and to recommend authoritative speakers on each from various traditions. They insisted, too, that we must find rank-and-file Christians as well as bishops and theologians, women as well as men; and in many cases the speakers suggested by the panel were eager to make further recommendations of their own. The planning of our itineraries – which involved almost a hundred appointments up and down the country was carried out by our researchers Patrick Forbes and Hugh Faupel.

The broad topics mapped out by our Four Wise Men were as follows:

1. The nature of Christianity
2. Who Jesus was
3. How we know God
4. God, man and sin
5. The meaning of the Cross
6. Christianity and other faiths
7. The Holy Spirit
8. The Trinity
9. The Church
10. Worship and prayer
11. Sacraments
12. The Christian hope
13. A summing up

Our advisory panel, though it should not be held responsible for what we ultimately produced, took a thoroughly positive view of what we proposed. 'Convergence' is the fashionable word for what is happening among the churches today and certainly the Anglican, Roman, Methodist and Presbyterian Wise Men came together with us in a perfect example of the harmony and humility that Chris Rees and I believed we should find among enlightened Christians in Britain. There was no anxious pushing of favourite dogmas, only a concern that we should not present any of them as claiming to have a cut, dried and packaged faith. Above all, they insisted that over the past thirty years there had been a transformation, a great opening up of relations between their churches which too often had not filtered down to the man in the street. To use the terms loosely, protestants had become more catholic and catholics more protestant, each seeing the point of what the others had once had to defend in an atmosphere of hostility.

'This is an exploration of mystery,' we were told. 'In saying we know about God we must make it clear that we know very little. Religion is not just an intellectual business, a product of the mind. It must not insult intellect, but it is much more than intellect. Nor is Christianity just about the individual being saved. It is community. We need also to stress that faith is a *response* to God. We must constantly say what we *do* about it.'

By the time we had completed our interviews, we had some forty-eight hours of questions and answers. Physically as well as intellectually it was exhausting. Towards the end my back was tormented by travel-fatigue (which a Scottish bishop's wife attempted to treat with the laying-on of hands), while Chris Rees had to take to his bed with a rare attack of trench mouth. His treatment was rather more effective than mine; but that is probably a reproach – and not the last, I dare say – to my lack of faith rather than that of the bishop's lady.

What it all did to our victims, they were too kind to say. A list of those we talked to is appended at the end of the book and I would like here to express my gratitude to all of them. Some may feel they went through a great deal and then found very little to show, or rather hear, for it. But even those from whom we extracted only a few sentences, or nothing at all, made their contribution to my pilgrimage.

Our thanks are due to those so often taken for granted in broadcasting: to the executives and planners who placed their confidence in us, to our administrators, secretaries, researchers and recording engineers. Thanks to all of these Priestland has, I hope, made some progress; though I must say I remain where I was, in the Society of Friends, that society now seems greater than I had imagined, and I have gained a far wider circle of friends.

One small accidental ritual, repeated everywhere we went, did more than anything else to confirm me in this. In order to enrich the stereophonic recording and cover any gaps left by editing, we concluded each interview by recording at least three minutes *of the silence of the room* – whether it was a bishop's study or a suburban front parlour. Every room has its own distinctive silence, though it is never completely quiet, what with birds tweeting, clocks ticking and traffic humming past. Almost a hundred times we explained our curious custom and told our victims that they were free to go and make tea or to join in our modest retreat as they pleased. Almost without exception they chose to stay; and I mean no disrespect to their eloquence when I say that it was usually the best part of the interview. What passed through their minds I have no way of knowing. For myself, I sat there, the three minutes getting shorter every time, putting from my mind my good thoughts as well as my bad ones and 'thinking only [as the medieval mystic puts it] that you are as you are and He is as He is'.

The response of listeners to the broadcast series (and its perky little signature tune) was overwhelming. All over the country study-groups were formed to follow it, and the audience for that time of night quadrupled. Our office was stacked with boxes of letters, all of which were read though it was physically impossible to acknowledge, let alone argue with, them all. I am afraid I offended those to whom Christianity is perfectly straightforward and all in the Bible. But to my joy I seem to have brought encouragement to what I call the Great Anonymous Church of the Unchurched: those who believe, or would like to believe, but are disenchanted with the churches and dare not discuss their faith elsewhere for fear of being thought neurotic or gullible. To them I say, Christianity is not a way of unreasonable certainty, it is a far more interesting way of reasonable uncertainty. Let us talk about it frankly and openly together.

CHAPTER ONE
By What Authority?

You might think the least important thing about a book or a programme is its title. Surely what matters is the content. And yet one fusses over the title for hours; as if, like the figurehead of some romantic merchantman, it conferred magical properties upon the ship and all who sailed in her.

In a more businesslike mood one worries whether the title will make people want to switch on in the first place. Will it attract them to the goods being offered? Might it even imply an ingenious excuse for their shortcomings, as in *A sideways look at Christian theology*? The suggestion of *Priestland's Progress* came as a relief after some of the more portentous alternatives, such as *I Believe, Pilgrimage of Grace, Towards Faith, The Road to the Cross* and *The Great Christian Teach-in*.

Priestland's Progress had flattering overtones of a plain man boldly marching across a landscape of hopes and heresies; but the slightly ridiculous effect of the alliteration should prevent it from sounding too awesome. If people found themselves humming 'Who would true valour see', so much the better; but by pinning the expedition to *me* we hoped to make it clear that this was not the only road, let alone the officially approved one, to the Celestial City.

If I was to be an honest pilgrim there was no certainty in what state I would arrive or whether I would get there at all. But where was I to begin? It seemed obvious that any investigation of Christianity should start with Christ. But our Four Wise Men had said no, the first thing to get straight was the question of what they called 'authority'. If we were going to spend nine and three-quarter hours talking about God we had better know where our ideas came from and what relative importance we should attach to them. For example, the doctrine of the Trinity – that God was somehow Three in One and One in Three – went back more than 1600 years and claimed justification from the Bible, which gave it a good deal more authority (in the sense of moral power) than the recent suggestion that Jesus was really a psychedelic mushroom. But why? If the mushroom idea were true the fact that it was a newcomer on the scene ought not to prevent it having just as much moral strength as the doctrine of the Trinity.

But this, in the context of the Christian faith, seems unlikely. If you look at the Church as a whole you find that it roots its authority in a soil compounded of scripture, tradition and reason – though some parts of it place more emphasis on one ingredient than another. To find the psychedelic mushroom in the scriptures requires a perverse ingenuity. It is certainly not in any tradition that has stood the test of time; and very few people find the mushroom theory reasonable. It is true, of course, that many people do not find Christianity itself reasonable; but even the Catholic tradition, which so often resorts to the term 'mystery' (a truth beyond the powers of reason to apprehend) insists that faith must be *consonant* with reason.

Clearly our first programme, if it was to establish authority, would have to begin by defining some terms: What was religion anyway? What was doctrine, and why was it necessary at all? Could we treat religious language, including theology, like any other form of talk with which people were familiar? How were we to handle the Bible?

Curiously, you may think, there was never any question of having to start by proving the existence of God. The most immediate reason for this was that by definition we were bound to be the converted preaching to the converted. I would love to tackle the question of God's existence some day (though how should I presume to compete with so brilliant an apologist as Professor Hans Küng?); but a series of programmes on the fundamentals of the Christian faith was hardly likely to come from or be aimed at anyone who considered its basic assumption to be nonsense. Speaking for myself, it is not so much that I *know* God exists or that I *believe* he exists as that I *trust* in Him, and find that trust continuously confirmed by experience. He is, if you like, the best hypothesis I have come across to explain the nature of the underlying reality of life.

In the past the Church has sought to prove the existence of God in terms of reasoned philosophy: Anselm tried in the ninth century, Aquinas in the thirteenth. But as Kant argued in the nineteenth century, since God appears to operate beyond the system of natural connections, His objective reality cannot be proved or disproved by speculative reasoning. I do not think there are many theologians today who would claim that philosophical – or scientific – 'proofs' can be relied upon. Most modern theologians would argue that in spite of science it is still possible to trust in God with a faith that rises above reason without denying it; and that this faith produces an understanding of reality which makes sense, which hangs together even though it has to confess its incompleteness. Often it is this absence of completeness, which the Church calls 'mystery', which leaves reason discontented, even outraged. And to reason's further annoyance it is this *understanding*, this *making sense* without necessarily giving a total explanation in terms of demonstrable knowledge, that theology is about. Philip Toynbee wisely observed, 'Theology is not about God but about Man seeking for God: Heaven guessed at from Earth.'

Some branches of the Church would insist their theologies were a great deal more than human guesswork – that they had divine authority. For myself, however, faith remains 'the assurance of things hoped for, the conviction of things not seen', and this involves a strong commitment of personal trust. A better Christian than I would maintain that my trust has to be in the person of Christ, who is God, and that God as the author of all things is the ultimate authority of His Church. There are those who have told me that the only way to know God is to go down on my knees, tell Jesus I accept Him as my Lord and ask Him to take over my life. The trouble is, I am afraid, that I am not like that. I can see that there are short cuts I could take on this pilgrimage, like leaping over chasms of doubt. But I really would prefer to take the longer way round, for there is some interesting scenery on the way.

The trust that underlies my faith is an example of this. It seems to me that while Jesus himself is indeed a person, He has been filtered down to us through many other persons; that the Church itself is and has always been *people*; and that while a centuries-old consensus of the faithful is less likely to be wrong than one individual hunch, such a consensus is not necessarily infallible.

I find that my faith, such as it is, depends heavily upon my trust in people, living and dead; a trust tempered by my judgment of the completeness or incompleteness of their insights. It follows that I must have the same attitude towards the Church. *Priestland's Progress* involves a long series of such judgments. I have been impressed by and come to trust some witnesses more than others; and I suppose that my judgment of them has been influenced by my personal background, by the sort of person I am. One's internal picture of the sort of person one considers oneself to be is a constant touchstone in all one's choices.

The point I am making here is that for me the Christian faith is very much a matter of trusting Christians, in a line stretching back to the person of Christ himself. Perhaps that is what is meant by 'the communion of saints'. But if I were to reach the conclusion, for example, that Jesus was indeed the unique Son of God, a powerful factor influencing me would be that people I had come to respect in personal encounter had convinced me of their own confidence that it was so. I think it would also have to 'make sense' to me (or, as Quakers say, 'speak to my condition'); but the subjective quality of respect would have much to do with it. One's respect can, of course, turn out to be ill-founded. You too, reader, will have to determine whether you respect and trust *me* as a result of our encounter in these pages.

Nor should you imagine that this is entirely a matter of reasoning, of catching me out in my arguments. For the Christian religion is emphatically not just an intellectual business. It is not a theory about God, but a response to Him. It is heart and guts as well as head.

It is easy enough for modern science to explain the need for religion. As Dr Jack Dominian, the distinguished Roman Catholic psychiatrist, puts it, we start life totally dependent upon our mother, develop our relationship with the outside world through our father and others close to us, and as we mature we reach on upwards towards some absolute source of love and acceptance. Unless we have such a source, human life tends to become meaningless.

Does such a psychological explanation invalidate religion, or render it mere wishful thinking? No, because the unrequited desire for God would not be enough by itself to produce faith. There has to be some answering revelation of God to make sense of our desire. God reaches down to Man as well as Man up to God; and for most of history heart as well as head has confirmed the reality of the encounter. There *is* a relationship, not a monologue addressed to some indifferent – or non-existent – principle. Which is why we speak of a personal God. It may well be that atheism is as much due to neglect of the heart as it is to cultivation of the head.

The veteran zoologist Sir Alister Hardy believes that the sense of the religious has been a vital factor in our evolutionary success; that by giving strength, spiritual power and comfort in times of distress, faith has brought a stability which is lost if religion is discarded altogether and dismissed as mere superstition and wish-fulfilment.

The popular belief that science has explained away religion is a tenacious one, indeed the official one in communist countries; yet it is as out of date as animal magnetism. In the Middle Ages, when knowledge was virtually reserved to the Church, theological systems dominated and the natural sciences (as Galileo learned to his cost) were expected to devolve from and confirm theology. Two unfortunate trends developed from their inevitable drifting apart. Religion believed it had found a new enemy (perhaps the most dangerous it had ever had), while science believed it was now liberated from any system of values other than the objective search for facts.

Dr John Habgood, Anglican Bishop of Durham, was trained as a scientist. He says:

Earlier this century I was very much oppressed by the way science was pointing us so firmly towards materialism. But the development of physics has put a very large question mark against that now. I think also the study of the history and sociology of science has raised some very awkward questions about what kind of an enterprise science is. There's been a certain loss of scientific self-confidence because of the moral and human problems created, a questioning as to what it is right to do with science. As soon as you begin that, you are treading dangerously near religious ground.

Now, a theologian must at some point make assertions about truth; while scientists have all these years been rather retreating from the question of truths and saying they are just handling the data. But if science goes too far along that road, it is going to find itself undermined by those who want to politicise science. Therefore I hope scientists will see the point here, that they have a common cause with theologians not to look at superficial correspondences, but to share a quest for the truth.

Professor John Bowker of Lancaster, who has devoted a great deal of study to the relationship between science and religion, points out there is no such thing as final science; it is always provisional and changing. At the moment he thinks we are living in a time when scientific reflection is reinforcing the validity of the religious quest. Professor Bowker thinks there are analogies to the Trinity in information theory; and he sees in what is known as entropy the key to our understanding of death.

What entropy means is that when you've used up energy to build something, though you never lose the energy, it can't be used to do that work again. There's a general flow of energy towards randomness and disorder. This helps us to understand death as sacrifice. The religious issue is whether we can acquire a sense that sacrifice is a necessary condition of any life at all. This is a tremendously profound insight which connects up with all religions, but especially with the figure on the Cross.

Bowker agrees that religion, too, is as provisional and open to correction as science: that it can never present us with the final and complete picture. We do not know, exhaustively, what the universe is all about or even who Jesus was. But the religious approach is based upon some very well tried and tested ways of being human. Real events have left their mark upon it. How we reflect on them, what we make of them, may be open to admendment, for there is very little we can actually prove. But the realities upon which we reflect will endure, and the religious approach will always pick itself up and try to repaint the picture.

This image of a faith that was far from complete, that was still pressing forward, was one offered by many of those I talked to; it shocked only a minority. If it needs biblical justification, that is to be found in the sixteenth chapter of St John's gospel: 'I have yet many things to say unto you, but ye cannot bear them now. Howbeit when he, the Spirit of Truth, is come, he will guide you into all truth . . . and he will shew you things to come.'

I must admit that I had embarked upon the series expecting to find a Church that was either smugly entrenched behind antique fortifications or despondently resigned to fading away. It was thrilling to discover nothing of the sort. I am thinking here less of those conservative evangelicals who trumpet that the Good News was the same as it had always been, that Jesus lived and was marching on in triumph. I am thinking rather of witnesses like John V. Taylor, Bishop of Winchester, with his insistence that the Church had barely *begun* to appreciate the inner truth: 'If you take the long view, perhaps it isn't so long, 2000 years. It could be that Christianity is only just beginning.'

What John V. Taylor is reaching for is not a secularised, scientised Christianity, still less an old-fashioned belief in some omnipotent potentate. He believes that the basic power beneath things is a weakness powerful only in the way that love is powerful, at the end of a long process of endurance, disappointment and vulnerability. In short, God's only power is love.

This is not an easy belief to swallow, and if it is true it may turn a lot of ideas on their heads. Taylor believes the Christian Church itself has helped to mislead people by seeming to endorse the idea of a potentate God and by chasing after power within its own structures. 'So it is not altogether surprising that what I believe is the central truth of Christianity is only just beginning to emerge.' With respect, I think traces of this approach have been around for a very long time indeed. It is certainly at the heart of the Jesus story. But it seems to me that Taylor is right when he seeks to turn us from shallow triumphalism or the reshuffling of old dogmas and make us confront the failures and defeats of the Kingdom.

Yet this has brought me into the field of what might be called experimental Christianity, and some way off the beaten track. When I asked John Stott, probably Britain's best-known evangelical preacher, what was the essential equipment of his type of Christian, he answered: 'An evangelical is primarily someone who believes the gospel, accepts the authority of the Bible, and believes that God accepts us in His presence not for any good works or merit of our own, but solely through the work of Jesus Christ when we come to Him in penitence and faith.' This was doctrine, clear and strong. I received equally strong and clear statements from other witnesses of different tendencies. But what was doctrine, and why should we need it anyway? If there was a God, he was surely so far above us that any attempt to define His ways would be impertinent and probably wrong.

John V. Taylor himself demurred at this. We must not scare ourselves with the thought of God's incomprehensibility. We might only see the tip of the divine iceberg, but we could still know God within our limits. Doctrine was important for two reasons. First, what we believed determined the pattern in which we saw the world around us. Second, we could not regard faith as purely an individual matter. Being a Christian must mean some degree of involvement with others who followed Christ, and among such people there was bound to develop a consensus, an orthodoxy, with which the individual was in dialogue. That was not unique to religious institutions. Scientific researchers only remained respectable if they stayed in dialogue with the scientific consensus, speaking its language impersonally and managing to convince it that they were not talking nonsense. Which left me thinking that conservative doctrine might be justified, even to a renegade like myself, as a useful critic of the new, or at least a wall off which new ideas could be bounced.

I doubt if that is what Cardinal Hume had in mind. It has sometimes been difficult to make out whether the Roman Catholic Church regarded scripture and tradition as separate but equal in authority, or whether it was insisting that tradition was superior (being necessary for the correct interpretation of scripture). Since the Second Vatican Council it looks as if the Roman Catholic Church is trying to say that the two are inextricably locked together; which is fair enough when you appreciate that scripture must be a product of tradition. Each of the four gospels, it can be argued, is based upon a certain tradition about Jesus.

My discussion with the Cardinal about doctrine could easily have been seized on by an ultra-protestant as typical of the rather dodgy way the Church of Rome appears to say one thing very firmly and then wriggles out of it. Technically, a person who formally denied one of the doctrines infallibly defined by the Church would be a heretic in danger of Hell. But, as Father Basil pointed out, there was the subjective aspect of diminished responsibility. People who through no fault of their own do not enjoy the fullness of the Catholic faith do not qualify as heretics.

Furthermore, since the definition of the doctrine of infallibility at the First Vatican Council (1870) there has only been one clear exercise of that authority by the Pope. It is true the earlier examples have never been rescinded (it is hard to see how they could be, if they claim to be infallible), but it is important to remember that when the Pope does make such a pronouncement he is not claiming to lay down the law as an individual acting on his own initiative – even one with contacts in unusually high places – but to define what the consensus of the faithful already is. In theory, at any rate, he is acting as the mouthpiece of the whole Church.

Roman Catholics would say today that while Christ's Church can be found in other churches – 'that they have got an awful lot right', as Father Basil puts it – it is there in a manner which is less than totally complete. The authority claimed by the Roman church rests on the contention that there is a continuity between itself and the original church of the apostles founded by Christ himself; from St John to Polycarp, from Polycarp to Irenaeus and so on through the Fathers of the Church who wrought its doctrine.

Father Basil observes:

The Roman Catholic Church is often accused of giving quick and easy answers to everything, but in fact we are a good deal more subtle. The Church takes a very realistic and compassionate view of the way human beings function. How many people would deliberately choose to do something evil without an enormous number of qualifying factors? In other words, the Church's moral law is one thing; but the pastoral judgment about how people live in accordance with it can be another.

This approach has its effect upon theological doctrine as well as moral law. The Roman Catholic Church does claim certainty upon a number of fundamentals to be found in the creeds. But it does *not* claim these tell us everything about God. It points to the closing verse of St John's gospel: that all the books in the world could not contain everything Jesus did. 'A very important statement,' says the Cardinal, 'because he's saying that even in the New Testament we haven't got the totality of what Jesus said and did, or a complete understanding of how He could be both God and man.'

John Bowker presented doctrine again in terms of communication theory. If the churches had truth to communicate – and most Christians believed that they were charged to do so – then that message had to be *protected*. It was not only a question of protecting it against misunderstanding and distortion of various kinds, but of insulating it against the competing noise of the world. It was rather like wrapping up a parcel in brown paper so that it did not come apart and get lost in the post.

I was still worried, however, about the nature of the religious language I was hearing. My own brief career as a part-time philosopher in the 1940s was heavily overshadowed by the school of logical positivism, which taught that theological statements had no real meaning since they could not be checked as true or false either by logic or experience. The attitude lives on in, for example, the work of

Sir Alfred Ayer. There is hardly room to do battle with it here, but it seems to me that the principal objection to it lies in the difficulty of accepting that so many intelligent people, for so many centuries, should happily have been talking nonsense without knowing it; and not merely talking and writing it but living it and, by their actions and experience, confirming its meaningfulness.

However, positivism and other varieties of philosophy that take the form of analysing what, if anything, we really mean by what we say do provide a healthy discipline against romantic waffle. There is no denying that if I say 'God is Love' I am not talking on the same level as when I say 'There's a cat in the garden'. I can confirm the latter by taking a photograph; but not the former. So is it meaningless when I – or, what is more important, Mother Teresa, St Thomas More and the author of *The Cloud of Unknowing* – say 'God is Love'? I think not. We all know what we mean and how we know it; and although the explanations might not satisfy a positivist, they would satisfy a great many other people of integrity and intellect.

The obvious way out is to grant that religious language is not the same as how-to-mend-a-motorbike language or even how-to-find-the-square-root-of-infinity language. We may use some of the same words but not with the same intentions or based on the same kind of experiences. The language of faith is more like poetry; some of it explicitly is poetry. It is full of metaphors and similes (the body of Christ, the fire of the Holy Spirit . . .) which we know very well do not literally correspond to what we are talking about. Poetry can convey the deepest of truths.

And yet to call religious language 'poetic' worries theologians because it may give the impression that they are not to be taken seriously. I have heard it argued that in the end religious language is more like scientific language than it is like poetry. Certainly that would have been the contention of a medieval schoolman such as Aquinas, who was as much a logician as a theologian. The trouble with the poetic approach is that it can become too far detached from what the Church insists are the basic facts.

Certainly religious language is creative. If often tries to say more than words will bear. Human words, tied to intellect, often fail to support meanings that are better carried by symbols, art, music or dance. That kind of striving, itself poetic, musical and symbolic, is to be found in the best of liturgy.

Michael Hare Duke, Bishop of St Andrews, thinks religion does best in using the language of stories, as Jesus so often did; for stories are never definitive, they are open-ended, one leading into another. 'I've always found it fascinating talking to rabbis: when you ask them for an explanation they never give it to you in philosophical terms – they simply tell you another story.'

Stuart Blanch, Archbishop of York, has had exactly the same experience:

You'll never find a Jew talking about theology. I was at a consultation recently at which this came up, and the Jewish representatives there renounced the word theology, because for them all religion is concerned with encounter, response and obedience. They're not interested in the kind of mighty intellectual structures built sometimes upon very slender foundations which have been so characteristic of the Christian Church.

How did it happen? Once Christianity broke out of Palestine and the narrowly Jewish circle of the apostles, it fell into some of the best minds of the pagan world, into the Greek view of things. All early theology was conducted on Greek premises, using Greek formulae, the Greek language and the concepts of Greek philosophy – concepts wholly alien to the Jews who had spent at least five hundred years resisting Hellenism and holding fast to the Jewish experience of the nature of God. The Church lost contact with that view, its own native view, and has been subject to abstract philosophical Hellenism ever since. Stuart Blanch was not the only witness who exclaimed: 'We must get back closer to the Jews!'

I heard the same cry from Donald Reeves, the maverick vicar of St James, Piccadilly: 'One of the reasons why Christianity has become such a superficial thing is that we have lost the Jewishness of our faith.' He links this with the ineffectiveness of modern theology:

We need theologians to help us reflect on our experiences of trying to create a just and caring society, for which the Church is there to offer its life. What we do *not* need is white, male, middle-class theologians writing books to each other in universities, in jargon which hardly anyone except themselves can understand. It's time they stopped writing books and started to work for the Church. They are the people who should provide the critical, prophetic part of the Church's ministry.

And yet a simple, prophetic People's Religion cannot be the whole story, it seems to me. Greece is a fact. It has helped to make us what we are; and there will always be an intellectual spearhead pressing forward and asking awkward questions which may not seem immediately relevant to the fishmonger of today, but may revolutionise the thinking of his priest tomorrow. Western man is like that, and it is no service to the faith for Christians to be naive. If the theologians and other talkers-about-God cannot keep up with the scientists and political theorists, the world will go secular and materialist, starting in the universities and working downwards.

Perhaps, to a considerable degree, that has already happened. After the first four or five centuries, Christendom entered a long period which was culturally very static. Throughout the Middle Ages scholars tended to look back with awe to the giants of classical Greece and Rome, and to preserve their wisdom in much the same terms and categories of thought. Professor Dennis Nineham (one of our leading modernist theologians) argues:

From the Renaissance on, we entered a period of galloping cultural revolution, which should have made it impossible to state the truth in the old terms. But after the experience of ten or twelve hundred years, Christians had got it deep into their minds that their faith consisted in believing, in more or less the identical words, what people had believed in the days of the Creeds and the New Testament. Understandably it has taken the Church a very long time to realise that this is no longer possible and that we have got to devise new formulations. We have to ask ourselves 'What must the truth be *now* if people who thought like that so long ago put it as they did?'

Working alongside Professor Nineham at Bristol is Denys Turner, a philosopher who took to theology because it seems to him to raise issues that are far more real than those he encountered in the world of academic philosophy. He says:

Philosophers are always worrying about appearance and reality. If a philosopher were to attend to the fact that every Sunday millions of people stand in front of an overdressed man, holding up a piece of bread and saying to them 'This is the Body of Christ', then it seems to me that philosophers' discussions would come very much closer to the way people actually live. Nobody takes seriously Wittgenstein's problem of whether the broom in the corner can talk. Whereas people do live their lives in deeply committed and serious ways around the belief that this piece of bread is the body of a dead man two thousand years old. That seems to me a real form of life which may possibly be illusionary, but it seems to me that the real illusions of life are very much in need of exploration.

'The real illusions of life' is a deliciously paradoxical phrase which comes very close to explaining what the sacraments are about.

How do such 'illusions' claim authority over Christians? Partly because the Church maintains it has had the tradition handed down to it in unbroken line. This is a form of the respect-derived-from-encounter – the trust – which I myself have felt during my Progress. But at the heart of that respect lies a record of encounter known as the Bible. Christianity and its Church would be nothing without it. Suppose that we had no scriptures: that the Church rested on nothing more than a series of carved representations of the Crucifixion and a tradition that the Son of God had been put to death by men two thousand years ago. What sort of religion would we have? Probably little better than desperate prayers to ward off God's punishment. We should know nothing of redemption and forgiveness. Only the Bible records that.

In every church it is accepted as being, in some sense, the Word of God. But it is not so in the sense that the Moslem Koran claims to have been dictated to Mohammed and set down, word for word, without any sort of human intervention. John Stott told me:

The Bible has the authority of God because God himself has spoken. Obviously that is a metaphor, but we believe that God has communicated himself progressively to mankind through the prophets, culminating in Christ, His own incarnate Word, and in the witness of the apostles to Christ. I do not believe that there could be a more authentic or authoritative witness to the historic Jesus. We may have more to learn, but I don't believe God has any more to teach than what he has once for all revealed in His incarnate Son.

I ventured to suggest that, while God might have spoken, he had done so, surely, through fallible human beings using inadequate human language. Stott did not quite like my use of the word 'fallible', but he agreed that the Bible had dual authorship, human and divine. The fact that it was the inspired word of God did not smother the humanity of its writers – their different styles and theologies – 'but the fact that it was written by human beings does not mean that obstructed the Word of God. Neither one destroys the other.'

Stott went on to say that we had constantly to *interpret* scripture in the light of the times in which it was written. When God became man, in the form of Jesus, He became a first-century Palestinian male Jew and spoke in a particular social, historical and cultural context. We could not understand His word detached from that context, and it was often painfully difficult to think ourselves back into it. So in what sense was the Bible true? Obviously it couldn't just be true because it said it was.

The Bible, said Stott, was true in the sense in which its authors intended it to be understood as true. To quote a modern American maxim, 'A text means what its author meant.' 'True' does not mean that all of the Bible is literally or historically true, for there are many dramatic figures of speech involved (said another witness: 'We have to remember the Bible is an *oriental* book'); and when it comes to the Old Testament we cannot expect to find the fullness of God's revelation there.

I came away from that encounter feeling I had been told the Bible was never false, but that it was often extremely difficult to be sure in what sense it was true. Indeed, one distinguished Oxford scholar told me he thought lay people would do better to leave the Old Testament well alone and concentrate on the New – preferably St Mark, and omitting St Paul entirely. That, I fear, was a bad case of academic élitism.

The notion that the Bible is *inspired* (that is, breathed into its writers by the Spirit of God), though it sounds a bit woolly, can be helpful here. A Salvationist, Major Ken Lawson, said he believed the Bible to be inspired 'in the sense that God has communicated with people throughout the ages, and what we have is an unfolding awareness of Him'. He went on: 'And there is the other side to inspiration: not just the inspiration and understanding of those who write the Bible, but also of those who read it. Unless there is inspiration on both sides, it doesn't work.' This, it seems to me, is an intuitive substitute for the scholar's knowledge of the cultural background. It may be difficult, but not impossible, for the plain man to see the point of what St Paul is saying.

That was the experience of Stuart Blanch long before he became a divinity student. He, like others before and since, simply read the Bible and was filled with the conviction of its authority and importance. 'I would have said, if this isn't true – nothing's true. It was a revelation.' He, incidentally, argues strongly for the Old Testament, saying that a great deal of our misunderstanding of the New Testament over the past hundred years has been due to our failure to take seriously the Old. But he also makes the point that 'truths' are sometimes extracted from the Old Testament that are not in fact there: for example, the supposed prophecy of the Flight into Egypt which was never intended as a prophecy at all.

No one agrees more heartily than the Jews. The two rabbis whom I consulted on my Progress complained – not bitterly, for they were far too charitable – about Christian exploitation of their Torah (Genesis to Deuteronomy), which is highly selective. Stuart Blanch admitted that 'the Church has simply treated the Old Testament as a kind of quarry for texts which we hurl at our enemies'.

Rabbi Hugo Gryn cites the example of the 'eye for an eye, tooth for a tooth' doctrine for which Jews are often reproached. 'If you are scholarly, you will appreciate that this was a great advance in the administration of human justice. Because what it says is *only* an eye for an eye, not a life for an eye, which is what had applied before.' Gryn argues that the gospel accounts of the trial of Jesus do not make sense in Jewish terms: in law, His alleged blasphemy was no blasphemy and no Sanhedrin would have met on a festival night to condemn a man to death. Incidentally, Gryn also reproaches Christendom for its censorship of Jewish documents which (he believes) must have removed many contemporary references to Jesus which we would all have valued today.

Rabbi Lionel Blue, my other Jewish witness, brings up one very important criticism of the New Testament: its latent anti-semitism.

I join my Christian friends and sit back feeling well-disposed – dare I say quite Christian? – and then you get one of those awful remarks about the scribes and pharisees, my own saints and teachers, and really I feel quite battered. Do you realise what harm those statements have done? Because underlying modern political anti-semitism, say in Eastern Europe, there was a layer of Christian anti-Judaism. A vision goes through me of all those who got murdered, including my own relations, and of the pogroms that used to take place at Easter. And it's not very easy being detached about it.

Is the Bible true in the sort of texts that so distress Rabbi Blue? Were they inspired by God? No doubt they mean what their authors meant. But surely we have to place that meaning very firmly in the context of its time, when Christians were the persecuted underdogs, and ask ourselves Dennis Nineham's question: 'What must the truth be now, if people who thought like that put it as they did?'

Perhaps we should be careful of becoming, as many modern Christians do, too obsessed with the New Testament. It was Professor Robert Davidson of Glasgow who pointed out to me that the Old Testament, in its Jewish wisdom, makes a more honest attempt to face doubts, give voice to complaints and query religious certainties. The trouble with the New Testament, he observed, was that it came to us as the survivor of a limited age; whereas the Old Testament was the product of a long haul across the centuries. It would be wrong, he thought, to come to it through the New Testament; we had to appreciate it in its own right. 'I think, in a sense, the New Testament needs the Old far more than the Old Testament needs the New.'

The authority of the Bible, then, must be an authority not merely to take things at their surface value, but to think on these things. That is inevitable, if only because the Bible is not always consistent: it even conflicts with itself on points of detail here and there. And when it comes to theology, there is not one but many. Matthew offers us one interpretation of Jesus, John another, and St Paul a constantly developing theology drawn out of him by the pastoral problems of widely scattered Gentile congregations.

Father John Fitzsimmons, a Scots Catholic theologian, urges:

To keep your balance you must not concentrate on one to the exclusion of the others. Each may give you a different insight, and if you concentrate upon any one it does lead, obviously, to the kind of doctrinal differences we do experience. But my contention is that the more you get behind the formal doctrines and see the original insights, they can all be reduced to different ways of getting at the same truth.

Getting at the truth, then, is what the Bible is for; but we, its readers, still have to do the getting. The truth is there, waiting for us with authority, because the truth is contained in Jesus who was the Word of God in the supreme sense; because (as Christians believe) He was the supreme expression, communication and knowledge of God. Among all those words, outreaching their capacity, stands the Word. Which sounds high-flown – incomprehensible to any good positivist.

Graham Cray, a York evangelical, puts it more simply:

I don't believe that to be a Christian you have to believe that every word of the Bible is literally true. I don't believe, either, that it's full of mistakes. But I do believe the culture in which it's written has to be understood and the nature of each piece of literature. But above all, it's about Jesus and my faith is in a person, not in words in a book.

CHAPTER TWO
A Case of Identity

A person, not words in a book. But who *is* that person? The enquirer turns immediately back to the book, or rather to that library of books which make up the New Testament. To complicate matters, he or she finds that they are not just the same story told by four different reporters. They are not even 'reports' in the journalistic sense, but collections of sayings and deeds compiled retrospectively to back up certain points of view about Jesus; and they are full of borrowings from each other and from outside sources, of interpolations, improvements and censorings. Reading them, the enquirer finds not one Jesus but several: Jesus the prophet, Jesus the Messiah of Israel, the healer, the sacrifice, the second Adam, the Incarnate Word, the very Love of God. Each of us can impose a Jesus of our own. And yet common to all of these must have been a single human being with a real face and voice and body.

For there is no question of Jesus having been a fable, in the way that such heroes and demi-gods of the ancient world like Hercules, Mithras and Krishna were fabulous. They may have been based upon real people, but the records of them are nowhere near as immediate. References to Jesus in pagan literature are not very numerous – perhaps half a dozen, though many more must have been destroyed as too unflattering or heretical when the Church came to power. But there are still too many independent references to Him for there to be any doubt of His real existence. The difficulty for the historian is that the meaning of what Jesus said and did so overwhelmed His followers that they thought it quite unimportant to record much in the way of humdrum detail. What we have in the gospels is reverential literature, even propaganda, not contemporary journals. Nobody went about first-century Palestine with a notebook, or kept the diary of an obscure Galilean preacher.

I tried, throughout my Progress, to commence each stage

by recording as honestly as I could what I found I believed. Contemplating the whole question of authority, I found that I had no doubt of the existence of a personal God with whom there was two-way communication. What I did doubt was the reliability of the Bible as the key to understanding His will and His nature, and of the Church (in all its ramifications) as a guide to that understanding.

I emerged from that leg of the pilgrimage not comforted by new certainties but greatly reassured by the *uncertainties* that had been confessed to me. The Church claimed to know various things, and with its long history of worrying at them it was more likely to be right than I was; but even its creeds and dogmas were no more than starting points. Most churchmen considered that in Christ the fullness of God's reality had been revealed to us, but they insisted that their understanding of that revelation was very far from being complete – indeed, that human understanding was too limited ever to be complete. Whereas I had once mocked the Church for taking refuge behind the word 'mystery', I now saw it as an example of the Church's honesty. From my point of view the Church had gained in respect, therefore in trust, therefore in authority. And so had the Bible, since nobody was insisting I had to accept it simplistically. As a journalist, the older I grew the more complex I found the question of truth to be: I was relieved to find the Church agreeing. I was also relieved to find that I could keep saying 'the Church', without having to divide it up constantly into segments. There were differences of emphasis here and there, and the Roman Catholics and Orthodox clearly believed that each had something the others hadn't got. But all believed in the existence of one great overarching Church, and none was consigning the others to hell-fire. Most touchingly, the Catholics insisted upon the supremacy of individual conscience – while delicately observing that some consciences were more educated than others.

When it came to considering the figure of Jesus, I had to confess that statements like 'He was divine – the only Son of God' were not in my religious language. I was perilously close to the attitude deplored by our Four Wise Men, that of saying, 'Jesus was a very remarkable man, probably the most God-*like* there has ever been. But as to saying *He was God* – that's going too far.' I had been brought up, literally at my mother's knee, to pray 'Jesus, tender shepherd, hear me: Bless Thy little lamb tonight . . .' But now that I was more supernaturally aware than I had ever been as a child, my prayers were addressed to God – the Father, I suppose. I was *His* lamb. Admittedly, my awareness of God would have been very primitive without the example of Jesus. It was as if God had been saying, 'I am like this. I am *so* like this that as far as you are concerned I *am* this.' But an ambassador is not the king. An example of the artist's work is not the artist.

It is easy to see the Quaker influences in my personal image of Jesus, though I could not say which came first, the image or the Quakerism. As I read it, the mission of Jesus was the prophetic and pastoral one of trying to establish a holy people under the God of Israel. His message was that the Kingdom is upon us *now*, not in some time yet to come; that our sins are forgiven *now* if only we will acknowledge our need for forgiveness and reach out to take it. This was a revolutionary message, intolerable to any regime which had come to depend upon fear, hierarchy and ritual for its survival. And because of the times He lived in, Christ's mission was constantly assailed by efforts to politicise it and turn it into a liberation movement. This made Him still more of a troublemaker from the Establishment's point of view. His encouragement of the poor and disreputable, His disparagement of the pious and respectable, clinched the matter. He was rocking the religious and political boat by His absolute refusal to compromise with the power and hypocrisy which stood in the way of His Kingdom. And so He was tried and executed – the religious charge of blasphemy being converted into a political one for the benefit of the Romans. The death He died was deliberately designed to be humiliating and deterrent.

The manner in which Jesus accepted death presents Him to me as, above all, the Christ of non-violence. He and His followers could have avoided or resisted arrest; some of them tried to. But Jesus himself chose to fight by surrendering. It is not just that He absorbed the evil, stopped it in its tracks by renouncing bitterness and vengeance. By accepting the Cross He decisively ruled out any question of an earthly politicised Kingdom; and by removing His physical presence forced His followers into their personal discovery of the Spirit of God which flows through all of us. I still do not fully understand the Resurrection. It is possible that the disciples came to recognise that Jesus lived on in all of them. But I think it more likely that something objective happened, so powerful that it drove the young Church on to triumph against all the odds.

That is how I saw things at the beginning of this stage; and I have to say that while my experiences on the way have added to it, they have not caused me to delete very much. However, I must admit that it is an image of Jesus not based on any systematic study, and that it skims over some very awkward questions. Why are Christians, as a whole, so convinced that the death upon the Cross achieved something called salvation? How can they be so sure that Jesus was more than just the greatest and most influential man who ever lived? What can they mean by their assertion that He is alive with us still?

For some evangelical Christians the answer is simple, if huge: only *believe*, only make the leap of faith, and you will find that it is true. This is rather more than saying, 'It is true because I want it to be true', since in their experience you cannot imagine what it will be until you get there and find that it works. But, as I confessed, that isn't a path I feel I can take. One learns more from a problem by working at it laboriously than by guessing the right answer first time. In any case, I have already gathered that I am not going to get a final answer: the working out and the direction in which it leads me will probably have to do.

I must begin with the obvious fact – immediately jettisoned by most rank-and-file Christians – that Jesus was a Jew and thought of himself as one throughout His life. Rabbi Hugo Gryn, having reread the gospels in preparation for our conversation, said he could find no evidence anywhere that Jesus ever wanted to secede from the faith of Israel or to create a wider Church. To claim the title of a Son of God was no more than many Jews did.

My other rabbi, Lionel Blue, observed that for a Jew to claim that he was not only the *unique* Son of God but God Himself was both impossible and blasphemous.

Judaism can certainly think of the Spirit of God filling a person; of a person being open to God. It can think of a people being Children of God – hath not one Father created us? But the idea of the Incarnation is both the weakness of Christianity from the Jewish point of view and – in a strange sort of way – its strength. As for Jesus calling Himself Son of Man – Jews do regard themselves as paradigms of the human situation, and I can imagine Jesus thinking of himself as being the essence of the human situation in a nutshell; and therefore he's not just one man.

Hugo Gryn continued:

Up to that conference of apostles in Acts, chapter 15, there were no Christians separate from Jews. And then you get this conference in Jerusalem where the question is: are we Jews or not? And the answer is we're not. From then on there is a systematic attempt, particularly in the three late gospels, to make a very negative case against Jews and Judaism, to show that the new faith is superior and therefore the old faith was inferior, which in my opinion is entirely unfair and quite untrue.

The fact that Jesus was a Galilean, speaking Aramaic, suggests to Rabbi Gryn that He was a strongly nationalistic Jew who would have been troubled by three things. First, by the political effects of the Roman occupation, which had created a great deal of hardship and oppression. Second, by conditions within Jewish society; for there was a corrupt priesthood and the reform movement of the Pharisees was showing this up. Third, by the experimental mood of Jewish spiritual life as expressed by sects like the Essenes and Zealots. 'When the three come together, what Jesus suggests to me is an enthusiastic, deeply worried Jewish patriot, anxious to realise the historic mandate of God's Kingdom here on earth, and running into all kinds of difficulty on the way. I recognise in him a fellow Jew.'

Much of this is educated guesswork. The compilers of the gospels had other things on their minds than politics, Jewish social problems and obscure discredited sects; so they do not greatly help us. Indeed, they are so little help that for much of this century it has been fashionable to say that we can know very little about the real, historical Jesus. Our earliest evidence about Christianity comes from the letters of Paul. These cannot begin earlier than eighteen or twenty years after the Crucifixion, and while they show how quickly a far-from-simple faith had developed, they are maddeningly silent about the details of Jesus' life. Paul assumed his readers knew them from other sources, and in any case he had no eyewitness contributions of his own to make. Even the compilers of the gospels – which were probably composed between AD 50 and 100 – had to reconstruct certain episodes like the Nativity by treating passages in the Old Testament as prophecies which must have been fulfilled. For example, it is less than certain that Jesus was really born at Bethlehem, unless we accept Micah, chapter 5, verse 2, as fact rather than forecast; and even more doubtful whether Isaiah, chapter 7, verse 14, refers to the Virgin Birth.

So what *do* we know? We know at least more than our forefathers, thanks to painstaking textual scholarship, the occasional discovery of new manuscripts, and to archaeology. There are some enthusiasts who maintain we are learning something crucial from the growing authenticity of the Holy Shroud of Turin, with its striking image of a crucified man crowned with thorns and scourged; but this has always seemed to me a kind of holy red herring, incapable of telling us anything more than we have been told already. Others again swoop upon various apocryphal and gnostic gospels which claim to have secret knowledge suppressed by the Church. But invariably these are later than the four canonical gospels which we all know, and they are even more lacking in facts and coherence. The gospel of Jesus was never as simple as some bible-thumpers of today make out – it was constantly baffling the disciples, as we can read. It was a difficult message at times; but it was not cryptic.

Always we are driven back to the New Testament. The

basic story is this: Jesus was the oldest child in the family of Mary, wife of Joseph, a carpenter and possibly small builder of Nazareth. There was a family of at least five brothers and two sisters, and during Jesus' lifetime there seems to have been no suggestion that His parentage was other than it appeared to be. He was clearly fascinated by His religion and picked up a more than superficial knowledge of it; but He was not formally a scribe or a rabbi. Nor does it seem from His own teaching that He belonged to the austere Essenes or the terrorist Zealots; though he may very well have joined for a time the movement founded by John the Baptist.

John was a desert ascetic, a renouncer of the world and of orthodox piety and a prophet of the approaching Last Judgment. Frequent ritual washing was a characteristic of the Essenes, who were also awaiting the Last Days. But the baptism used by John was a different matter. It was intended to be a once-for-all-time rebirth of the penitent, to preserve them from the wrath of the Mightier One who was yet to come in judgment. All the gospels agree that Jesus himself underwent this baptism. The tradition of the Temptation in the Wilderness has strong overtones of the Baptist's way; and it is notable that while the gospels show the disciples of John and Jesus continuing separately, the Baptist was clearly respected among Christians.

It may have been the imprisonment of John that sent Jesus off on his mission. But instead of calling the people into the wilderness – the ancient birthplace of Israel – He went to them in their daily life in lakeside towns like Capernaum, where He may even have owned a house. He led a busy social life (which won Him an ill reputation among the orthodox) and He travelled the district preaching in local synagogues and, less formally, in the open air.

Jesus was a poet and story-teller who impressed His hearers by His readiness to speak on His own authority and not merely as an expounder of texts. Part of His skill lay in the fact that His teaching was cast in such *memorable* form. His tales, verses and epigrams were hard to forget and so easy to record reliably. Galileans were known as a superstitious lot, firm believers in miracles, and Jesus also won a reputation among them as a wonder-worker and healer. He obviously had a profound knowledge of human nature, for many of His cases were examples of what today would be called psychosomatic or hysterical illness, though the cures are no less remarkable for that. He had a particular sympathy for the poor and disreputable, in whom He seemed to find a greater honesty than among the pious and respectable: for He was careless of the social conventions and sarcastic about the rituals of righteousness.

His powers of leadership cannot be doubted. They enabled Him to recruit an inner core of disciples – a dozen, probably symbolising the twelve tribes of Israel – who were prepared to leave their families and possessions and follow Him. For the most part they were peasants and fishermen inexperienced in religious disciplines; and although they were sent out by Jesus to spread His message, I find it hard to see them as ordained bishops in a church of hierarchies. In the passage of time a Church was inevitable, but it could not have been Jesus' original work.

The heart of Jesus' message was that the Kingdom of Heaven – God's reign on earth – was at hand. On second thoughts, I believe Jesus was not quite saying it was actually there and then, though it was 'within you – among you'. It was, perhaps, in the process of breaking through and could only be brought fully to birth if people – and I am sure Jesus meant here God's ancient and holy favourites, the Jews – would repent. Ever since Moses they had had their special treaty with God, their Covenant, but constantly they had betrayed it, and look how low that had brought them! It was time for a new and quite different sort of covenant; not one of power in exchange for ritual observance, but of inner peace and reconciliation in exchange for spiritual honesty.

Repentance, He said, meant abandoning the illusion that entry to God's Kingdom could be gained by one's own efforts at being righteous. It meant acknowledging the need for God's forgiveness and opening one's heart to the free gift of God's love. There was more than a hint in Jesus' voice that time was running short and that the Last Days were round the corner.

If Jesus was wrong about that, then the Church, in a sense, is a magnificent salvage job. Dean Peter Baelz is one of those who thinks He actually was mistaken, and that He was not talking of some inner Kingdom. On the other hand another scholar, Francis Glasson, insists that there is no trace in the gospels of any supposed apocalyptic tradition, or that Jesus was influenced by it. There are many more, however, who see in the Jewish ferment of the times a lively expectation that a great crisis was approaching when God would intervene decisively in the battle between Israel and her enemies, and would do this by sending her a new king, the Messiah, to lead her. To most Jews that leadership would take the form it had in the past: military leadership.

Professor Robert Davidson of Glasgow thinks this may have some intriguing implications for Jesus' title as 'the Son of God'. He told me, 'It is one of the titles in the Old Testament which is applied to the king of ancient Israel who sat upon the throne of Jerusalem. As part of the coronation service there was a ceremony by which the king became God's Son by adoption. The Messiah is simply the Anointed; and the ruling monarch was the Messiah.'

So, I suggested, 'Son of God' could mean the restored king of Israel? It could, agreed the professor, though it was hard to say what influences might also have been at work from Greek mythology and the mystery cults.

Certainly the King of Israel as the Son of God is implicit in Psalm Two ('I have set my king upon my holy hill of Zion . . . Thou art my Son, this day have I begotten thee . . .') but it is quite clear that St Paul, for one, saw Jesus as a great deal more than that. At the same time Jesus himself, as we hear Him in the gospels, was extremely modest about claiming the authority of Messiahship.

His mission to Galilee was not the success it deserved to be. Now came the turning point. The gospels tend to emphasise His final trip to Jerusalem as the fulfilment of prophecy in obedience to God's will; but it seems reasonable to suppose that Jesus, feeling that time was running short and that He was not being properly understood, determined to publish His message to Israel from the holy hill itself. His challenge to the religious Establishment, especially by His onslaught upon the Temple, marked Him out as a trouble-maker. Evidently the Romans agreed; for whatever happened before the Sanhedrin (and we have seen that there are puzzles about it) Jesus could never have been crucified without being convicted of some offence against Roman law. The reason may lie somewhere in the dangerous overlaps between Son of God/King of the Jews/Messiah.

There seems no reasonable doubt that after His torture by professional executioners, Jesus was well and truly dead. Nor that, within a few weeks, large numbers of people became convinced He had risen from the grave and had been seen alive again. And then He vanished for good. If that had been all, we would have had nothing more than a miraculous hero; but there was more. Even after His final disappearance His followers kept having the experience of His invisible presence among them, which they interpreted as His gift of the Holy Spirit. (My own understanding of Pentecost, with 'every man hearing them speak in his own tongue', is that it was an outburst of precisely the sort of ecstatic chanting we can hear among pentecostals today.) But there was more, too; because remarkably soon people began to ponder the significance of this Man Risen from the Dead, and of what He had said in His lifetime, and to see in His death something much more than the opportunity for a miraculous survival. The very fact that He had not simply resumed living as before indicated that he was not just another John the Baptist *plus*.

At first His followers assumed that He would be coming again in their lifetimes to save them from the coming wrath. The best they could do was to live quiet and respectable lives, avoiding immorality and caring for one another, and remembering their Lord in the communal dinners that had been a feature of His way of life. Towards the end, He had laid a special emphasis on this.

But long before the destruction of Jerusalem some forty years following the Crucifixion, Jews were spread all over the Mediterranean world; and the news about Jesus spread through them into Gentile cultures. Paul, who had begun life as a religious secret policeman commissioned to stamp out the Church, became its chief propagator. The original Jewish Church of Jerusalem became quite eclipsed by the mixture of Greek, Jewish and Oriental thought which developed from Alexandria to Rome by way of Asia Minor and Greece. St Paul's early advice to these churches is governed by his expectation of the approaching end; but as time goes by, it becomes more and more responsive to their non-Jewish ways of thinking and to their local evolution of the faith. In any case, it was becoming clear that the end was by no means nigh.

Yet one thing stood firm, and perhaps it is the key issue still: not that Jesus was but that Jesus is. Unknown thousands of martyrs died bravely and cheerfully in the confidence that this was so. In Chapter 5 I take up the question of what it was He really did on the Cross. What I am concerned with now is who was or is this Jesus of Nazareth? Was He divine? Was He God?

John McQuarrie, who as Lady Margaret Professor of Divinity at Cambridge University occupies the oldest theological chair in the English-speaking world, introduced me to the approach of the twentieth-century German, Rudolf Bultmann. Bultmann was sceptical of the New Testament, some of which he saw as myth, some as the creation of the early Church. He did not think we had very much authentic information about Jesus – which does not seem a very promising foundation on which to build a faith.

On the other hand Bultmann believed that in Jesus Christ one met the ultimate demand for love and sacrifice, and that this was where faith began – a faith that could not be either bolstered or destroyed by historical research. Faith was the *response* to the *demand* one met in Christ or in the preaching of His gospel. And so the question of who He *was* – either historically or metaphysically – was not terribly important; what mattered was that He *is* this figure whose ultimate demands are forced upon us. It was undeniable that many people had found in Him a new meaning for their lives, what was traditionally called 'salvation'. Only because of that might one go on to raise questions about His relationship to God.

Father Harry Williams (one of Anglicanism's most popular spiritual writers) would say Jesus was the Son of God only in the sense that we were all potentially sons of God.

I don't think He was unique. I think of Him as somebody whose relationship with His heavenly Father was realised to the full. In us, it's not to anything like the same degree. But I don't think of Jesus as different in kind to myself, but the same as myself, and showing me my relationship to my Father as it really is. I don't think He intended the doctrine of the Trinity to develop – being human, I don't see how He could.

When I asked Professor Nineham whether he believed that Jesus was God, he replied that in his view the New Testament itself did not really believe so. The idea that Jesus was the Yahweh of the Old Testament would have seemed absurd and blasphemous. But later Christian thinkers in the Greek tradition undoubtedly *had* said it. 'And since I no longer share the Greek philosophical context, I no longer want to say that Jesus was God in their sense.' Nor does Professor Nineham *worship* Jesus; though he might subscribe to the image of Him as a 'window onto God – a rather smaller window than some people's'.

Dennis Nineham and Maurice Wiles, the Regius Professor of Divinity at Oxford, were members of the group that shocked the more traditional English Christians a few years ago by publishing a book called *The Myth of God Incarnate*. In any other country it would probably have been regarded as pretty old hat. Wiles, in his rooms at Christ Church, Oxford, told me he thought the rumpus was largely the result of different understandings about how religious language functions. He himself sees it as 'drawing upon our human experiences by a process of imaginative construction and symbolisation, and letting them point *in the direction of God*'.

Professor Wiles remembers being asked at a press conference whether he would say – yes or no – that Jesus was the Son of God?

To think that it is a clear-cut concept which can be dealt with in that sort of way seems to me to be a total misunderstanding. Anybody who had read scriptural history and so on would know that the phrase 'Son of God' has so many different concepts, indicating one who is in a very special relationship to God, focal for other men's faith towards God. What our book was feeling after was something which would keep the positive implications of a great deal of the traditional religious language, but free people from thinking it had to be understood in ways which I honestly believe diminish the effective reality of Jesus for our continuing faith.

Across the Oxford quadrangle, Professor McQuarrie was not in the least upset by the word 'myth', though he thought Wiles and Company might have read their Bultmann more carefully.

I think that for a long time it's been realised that talk of incarnation – God sending His Son and so on – is a pictorial kind of language, not conceptual language, and, if one wishes to use the expression, it is a mythological language. Maurice Wiles talks about Jesus Christ as the 'centre of God's presence and action in the world'. I really cannot understand why he's not willing to call that incarnation.

Disagreements among the great minds of the Church are very gentlemanly affairs these days. But when I asked Dennis Nineham whether he was a Christian at all he answered rather crossly: 'I don't think you can come along and say a person is a Christian who believes that Jesus was God in the sense in which Athanasius said it in fourth-century Alexandria. We've got to define it in our own terms, and insist on that pretty firmly.'

Cardinal Hume offered, as it were, various degrees of being a Christian when he answered my own self-doubts by saying:

If you accept that Jesus is the revelation and manifestation of the Father, then you are a follower of Christ and so a Christian. If you move from that to asking in what sense is Christ God, then I would think you have to come in the end to making that act of faith which is recorded of St Thomas the Doubtful: 'My Lord and my God.'

Valerie Fisher, a Lancashire vicar's wife, answered simply:

He's God. He is every aspect of God that can be comprehended by my human intellect and my senses. There's an awful lot of the whole big aspect I cannot cope with – the whole idea is too tremendous for me. But Jesus Christ is that of God capable of being put into a human form; and so I relate to God when I relate to Jesus, and by so doing I become more human than I could possibly ever be on my own.

God, then, *and* human – expressed with that humble intensity I found in so many of my women interview victims. But Mrs Fisher combined the two with a directness that escaped most of the men. Kenneth Barnes, a Quaker, thought of Jesus as a kind of super-Shakespeare, a person of great genius gifted with tremendous insight into human nature, conveying His message about the world while at the same time being totally involved in it. But was Jesus divine? 'I'm not terribly worried about this. We are all of us potentially transcendent beings, and the transcendence is the experience of God.'

That is a tempting way out. Why worry about whether Jesus is God? Perhaps it is something we cannot really know, or which depends too much on the classic phrase used by Dennis Nineham, 'It all depends what you mean by . . .' Better leave Him as a kind of Superman, one is tempted to say.

One case for making up our minds was put to me by the Reverend Paul Bates of Winchester:

It seems to me there is a link between what you believe about Jesus – what emphasis you place on His divinity and His humanity – and what sort of Church you have, what changes are necessary in it. I would guess that with the majority of people in the pew it was the *humanity* of Jesus they don't accept. They're less happy with that than they are with His divinity. A view of Christ that emphasises Jesus the man is going to have all sorts of repercussions on the role of the clergy and of the church in the local community, and the man or woman who's been a loyal churchgoer all his or her life is going to find that difficult.

One phrase that Jesus used in description of Himself was, indeed, 'Son of Man'. Robert Davidson groaned when I asked him what Jesus could have meant: 'Volume after volume has been written on this. It depends where you pick up the Old Testament. In Daniel it seems to be a synonym for the Jewish community. Ezekiel is addressed by God again and again as simply Son of Man. In the Psalms it is just a synonym for man. It could simply mean the representative man.' John Stott narrowed the choice down: Jesus was echoing Daniel Chapter VII and claiming the glory of the Messiah.

We seem, then, to be little further forward. On the one side we have those who are satisfied with the tradition of the Church, that Jesus *was* God. On the other we have those who agree that there has never been anyone else *like* Jesus, but who are reluctant to see Him float up to the heavenly stratosphere and get lost in the clouds of the Trinity, pre-existence and the mystery of the Logos.

The solution should lie in the ancient formula that as God incarnate He was both fully God and fully Man; and yet rationally this is an impossible mouthful for any of us to swallow. History will not allow us to say that Jesus was solely God (for it records that He was indeed a real man). So it seems that either we must say He was just a very remarkable man; or we must give up the game altogether – which means leaving it to others; or, drawn by the conviction that we *can* do better than that, we must press on into the mysterious realm where we apprehend that there is something that language cannot contain.

Paul Oestreicher, canon of Southwark, confessed:

I cannot explain the mystery of how someone who is a human being just like I am can also be worshipped. And yet the more real the mystery has become for me, it isn't that Jesus has become more like God, but that all my brothers and sisters have. It is through Him that I recognise God in my neighbour – through Jesus I've discovered the uniqueness of everyone. And there was in Him a quality of willingness to be defeated and destroyed by His enemies, and to go on loving them, that alone made possible a new quality of life afterwards.

Was Oestreicher talking about anyone more than a very special man?

But so special that in Him those who loved Him were able to recognise something they had to call God; it was divine. If others have somehow come through this Jesus to share aspects of His holiness, that mysteriously makes us one with God. There is a sense in which every man becomes divine. I would not want to draw hard, dogmatic lines between the rest of humanity and this Jesus.

In a similar vein, Canon Ivor Smith-Cameron suggested, tactfully, that there was a little too much Jesu-olatry about. 'I don't think that Jesus primarily called us to Himself. What He did was to call us together *with* Him in doing His Father's will. Jesus is the key to our understanding of the nature of God; though God is greater (if we put it like that) than simply being limited to the person of Christ.'

As I understand Catholic doctrine – and it is shared by many evangelicals, too – this is more or less heretical. The Church teaches that Christ tells us all we need to know about God, and that we shall never discover anything about God that is not already contained in Christ. In this it is serving the security of its doctrine, ruling out weird private insights. And, heretical or not, I find this idea of Christ being all of God that can be expressed in human terms – all we know and all we need to know – yet of God being still greater than Christ, both helpful and realistic.

In a sense Jesus was *not* God: in a sense He was. He was not, because it is inconceivable that if there is a God He could be totally contained or expressed in a human framework. Yet He was God, because take away Jesus and I, for one, would hardly have a God at all. Jesus is the knot around the crucial questions of God. He is the painted window through which we can hardly see, so brilliantly does the light of God shine through it. There are other windows, but not so dazzling.

In any case, I have been cheating. The most important part of the evidence about Jesus is yet to come. In human terms He held in tension the ordinary and the extraordinary, the lowest humility and the highest authority: the divine man. But there is something more that the Christian faith claims for Him: that because of the Cross, He is the saviour of the world. Whatever that means . . .

CHAPTER THREE
The Mysterious Mover

Whatever it does mean to be the saviour of the world, my Four Wise Men advised that I should take a somewhat round-about route to the subject. My pilgrimage must take in, at the earliest opportunity, what Bunyan might have called the University of Revelation; a place much beloved of theologians and not – as one might have hoped at first glance – a kind of divine exhibition palace full of thunder and lightning and visions of fiery chariots.

No one has ever seen God (or at least, not since Moses spoke to Him 'face to face, as a man speaketh unto his friend'). So on what do we base all this talk about Him? How does He communicate with us, and how do we know it is Him; for quite a lot of people say that the signals we profess to pick up are just history or nature or wishful imagination. God, we say, moves in a mysterious way His wonders to perform. But if He is so mysterious, may there not be a totally different explanation to life, or none at all?

Examining my own conscience, I found I could only reasonably say that the Christian God hypothesis fitted my experience better than any other I knew. It was not simple, but then neither was life; and like life it was often agonisingly uncomfortable and full of terrifying gaps. If it was constantly straining to become airborne, to leave the ground of definable facts, so were my own apprehensions of the world about me. The Christian hypothesis was confirmed by people I had come to trust and respect (including the writers of the Bible), and by occasional flashes of what a plain man, if not a theologian, would mean by revelation. Those flashes included what I can only call religious experience.

Sometimes these flashes have been very like aesthetic experience: a few bars of music, a phrase of poetry, the first impact of a painting or an avenue of trees has given me a split-second glimpse of eternity, of reality, in a nutshell. But at other times I have gradually become aware of a verbal message – always very brief – just hanging in my head. Its meaning is never clear immediately, but there is no doubt of its importance or where it comes from, and in due course it turns out to be crucial. On one occasion it was 'If not you – who will?' And on another 'I've got something for you' (followed by a chuckle).

Experiences like this are far more common than you might suppose, though people don't usually talk about them. I know of one lady who was enormously comforted by the words 'You silly old kettledrum!' Dr Edward Robinson, of the Religious Experience Unit at Oxford, told me of another:

It was at a moment of great depression when her life had reached rock bottom and she didn't know what to do. She said it was as if the voice of the Lord came to her – although she did not hear anything, it was just a sudden and unmistakeable conviction – saying, 'Look, everything is all right. You must never forget this, that everything is all right.' This was not a specific message in so many words, she said, but it was as real to her as if she had been given a command.

Edward Robinson went on to say that was typical of many of the 'messages' he had investigated. People spoke with conviction of knowing a certainty beyond all words, and often their lives were altered by it totally and irreversibly. 'The classic case, of course, is St Paul, and there are many others far less dramatic. But then there are lots of people who will say they have never had a religious experience but that all their lives they have been aware of some force, guiding, controlling and perhaps even frustrating them.'

Sir Alister Hardy, who founded the Religious Experience Unit, maintains that as many as half the adult population have had such experiences, though they may not belong to any institutional church; and that if only we could 'get back' to religious experience, we could arrive at a religion which was free of dogma and capable of adjusting itself to change, just as science does.

I find this approach very tempting, for the radical, mystical tradition in which I stand has always sought to cut out the middle man and make its direct connections with God. But without some discipline being applied there are considerable dangers in it. For a start it is isolationist. Not only is the Christian faith, as defined by its Founder, a community; but unless you expose your revelations to the community you run grave risks of deceiving yourself. One has only to think of Peter Sutcliffe, known as the Yorkshire Ripper, claiming that God had commanded Him to kill prostitutes to realise how grave these risks can be. The Church would insist that any private revelation must satisfy such tests as: Does it sound like the God we know of from other sources? Does it unite, rather than divide, the faithful? Does it have a visibly good effect on the one who receives it?

But although there have been some striking examples of private revelation, ranging from Joan of Arc's voices to the visions of the Virgin at Fatima and Lourdes, these are the ornaments rather than the building blocks of the Christian religion. Prophecy, mystery and the arts may also express God to us. But the most accessible routes, according to the Church, are creation and history.

Here, at once, atheists will complain that the Church is inventing an invisible gardener to account for a perfectly natural jungle. Bishop John V. Taylor of Winchester is well aware he is annoying them when he insists:

Quite a lot of their experiences, which they acknowledge to be real, are what I mean by God. If God is God, he is likely to be the most common of human experiences: people keep bumping into Him all the time, but that is not what they call Him. I think the Church has helped to create a division by giving the impression that religious experience is an exceptional and spooky thing.

The drift of this chapter so far has been that God is within us and to be known within us; and there is a great deal of Christian witness to that. But it runs the risk of making Him both limited and subjective – purely *immanent*, to use the theological term; and the objections remain if we enlarge it to mean that God is not merely in us, but pervades the whole created universe. So the counterblast comes, No, God is *transcendent*: He is outside, before and above anything created, not limited to time and place as we are, and beyond our understanding. Fortunately the official solution is that God is both immanent *and* transcendent. Harry Williams puts it: 'God is from one point of view infinitely other and infinitely greater than I am. From another point of view He is my deepest self; He is what I am.' Other Christians would say that the importance of Jesus was in reconciling the immanence and transcendence of God by being both God and man.

I find it easier to think of God as coming from outside and *flowing through* us and the universe. And that flow – the free and unearned gift of His love – is grace. So both God within and God without – immanent and transcendent – made possible by grace, the flow of His love. This is important in the matter of how God is revealed in creation and history, if I may borrow again from Father John Fitzsimmons to explain how: God the completely other moves out of the mystery of Himself and communicates with humanity in deeds and words. The very appreciation of that, our awareness of God, puts Him within us. 'The basic idea of the theology of grace – whether it's on the Reformed side or the Catholic – seems to me to be trying to explain the same thing: the impinging of unlimited God upon limited man, to the point where the transcendent does become immanent, where the Kingdom of Heaven is within.'

Maybe we need a deep breath at that point. But it is not going to last long, because unless we are careful we are going to come a cropper over the word 'creation'.

To some fundamentalists this will mean little more than the first three chapters of Genesis and a chance to knock down the theory of evolution. The point of knocking it down is to establish the literal truth of the Bible, including original sin, and to draw a neat line from the first Adam to the second (Jesus) without any tiresome questions about why the Creator apparently made so many false starts. Others, less fundamentalist, will want to see in the opening statements of the Bible a great tableau symbolising God's coherent establishment of all things and of man's stewardship of them.

But 'creation' has to do with much more than origin of species. In theological terms it means the continuing created order, without which there would be no means of knowing God and nobody to know Him. It means material nature and it means us too, since we are part of nature. Indeed, we are the pinnacle of it, since (as Genesis itself indicates) we have unique faculties which include the ability to know God and to sin.

What if there was *no* beginning to it all, as a conscious act of God? What if it was a meaningless accident? This again can be neither proved nor disproved. But if matter had a beginning that was beyond and before matter, that seems to me to take us into a realm of being which we may as well call God's. If it had none, then it seems to me we arrive in much the same realm by a different route.

Bishop John Habgood believes the doctrine of a Creator God means that we must look at the world as having a meaning which is discernible. It means, too, that we can look at it with gratitude as a gift. We should view it with a sense of responsibility, as something which is not merely there as a set of brute facts but as something entrusted to us. In more philosophical terms, to believe in Creation was to believe that the world was not self-explanatory, so that we were looking to a reality which transcended the world as we experienced it; a reality in which we could find its ultimate meaning and explanation.

How to answer the atheist objection that this was a mere imposed meaning?

I think one discovers that in a curious way the world can receive such meanings and answer back meaningfully. The growth of Christian experience over the centuries can be interpreted as some sort of conversation of faith, where people have learned to trust that the world has a meaning, and so have found one. Now you can say this is all fantasy; but the non-believer is then left with some rather difficult questions when he looks at the oddity of existence.

I ventured: 'So this business of responding and answering builds up? One begins to apprehend and trust there is a meaning, and one gets back an even richer response in the opposite direction?' 'Yes, that's exactly it,' said the bishop.

Has this something to do with those people who tell you

they find God most surely in their walks on the Cornish cliffs or the Lakeland fells? 'I feel very deeply about them,' said Canon Ivor Smith-Cameron.

There was a time when it wasn't thought proper Christianity to talk like that. I'm afraid the Church very often begins at a point far beyond people's natural experiences and ties up their sacramental life in a plastic bag. I want people to talk about their natural experiences of God. I want a larger and larger dose of what's called natural theology.

Creation, in the Christian tradition, is itself an act of grace – an expression of God's love. Everything exists in its own right and not as a divine plaything. There is no room for the belief that matter is evil; for evil comes from choice and only mankind (and angels, if you can find them) possess free will.

Creation was not once for all time. It is a continuous process, and as it continues towards its goal (which we can barely guess at) its unfolding is history; and the Church insists that this, too, is full of creative acts revealing God to us, if only we will reflect upon them. That, of course, is what the Old Testament is about; Israel never had any doubt of it. We see in it also, as commentator and judge on God's behalf, the figure of the prophet, not foretelling (which is quite another profession) but telling forth to society the truth about what it is doing and where it is going. Prophets are seldom accorded universal recognition: you might almost say that rejection was their badge of office; but I am advised you can tell them by their relevance to the whole community rather than to a few, by the compelling directness of their speech, and by their own faithfulness to what they preach. There are not too many of them about these days.

So God reveals himself through history? But when one looks through history it often seems a terrible mess, not a very flattering picture of our Creator. Says Professor William Shaw:

I don't see Him active in the sense of turning up to win a battle for one side rather than the other, or to cause an earthquake. I think God can only act through people and through their response to

Him. That does not mean He is not active all the time. I would want to treat creation in a very large framework, including not only His action in history through the prompting of individuals, but much more His dynamic relationship with the world of Nature.

Michael Hare Duke, Bishop of St Andrews, posed the mythical Father Kelly's question of 'What is God doing, if anything?' and brought in a Japanese tag.

Think of the inefficiency of a God who takes forty years of wandering in the wilderness to get His people from Egypt to Israel. The American marines could have done it in a fortnight. But it is the inefficiency of a loving parent who makes it possible for His children to grow by acknowledging His own weakness and giving them room. Powerful controlling parents usually produce pretty desperate kids because they do it all *for* them and there is no room for the kids to be anything but failures.

Bishop Hare Duke went on:

You see the inefficiency of God in the whole process of human history. Within it I continually find stories that say 'That's God'; though I recognise them looking backwards, I never know beforehand where He's going to arrive. I have no sense that He is guaranteed in, say, the actions of the British Prime Minister. He seems to me to be around in the Kremlin and all sorts of places, but I can't go along with people who say that God's in charge and therefore the person you meet at the bus stop was *meant*. That makes us simply all puppets. The fact is, we're here to grow and that's a messy business.

But basically I remain an old-fashioned liberal. I do think we are growing. I feel positive about the world – as well as dead scared. The nuclear possibilities make my stomach turn over. But nevertheless, given enough time, there's an astonishingly positive feel about the whole sweep of human history.

'You can really see a progress, onwards and upwards, taking place?' I asked dubiously. 'Given the fact that man has only been around for some five minutes in twenty-four hours,' said the bishop, 'I think we have achieved a great deal, besides making many mistakes. As I look back over

51

history I see more understanding about the need to love – though not an achievement of it yet. Still, I do believe there is an Omega point and that the whole process is going to get there.'

William Shaw resumed:

I think the implications are that God is very much nearer to us than we think, that He is confronting us at every moment with various possibilities, and that it really is He who is doing this. As a Christian, I claim to have some inkling of His intentions, which I believe the Church sees in Christ and which are His intentions for the whole of humanity and all of His creation.

Perhaps the most significant thing to have emerged from this leg of the pilgrimage is the insistence that God acts in history *through people*. That should be obvious enough, seeing that nobody pretends that he rides about the world, beard flowing in the wind, crying 'Stand aside, I'll fix that!' – though it would be easier for atheists if we did believe that, and frustrating for us if He did. However, to say that God acts through people does not mean, either, that when good chaps do good things we all say they are becoming God. The word 'response' is all-important. The good chaps are responding to God's grace, to the gift of God's love which is flowing through them. And I would recall here John V. Taylor's image of 'the sudden insight, the penny dropping' in quite ordinary situations. That is God acting in history.

Alongside this I would lay that other image of God's inefficiency, vulnerability, weakness. Spike Milligan – who is undoubtedly a prophet, if no theologian – demanded:

Why should we think God is perfect? By the look of things around us, things are very imperfect. If this is the creation of a perfect being, He's not working very hard. The imperfections are so manifest He must be imperfect. He's having a hard time. He's saying 'God Almighty! What am I going to do next? Riots in Brixton – none of them go to church – there's no preachers among them – the priests don't hold up bibles, they hold up truncheons . . . What can I do now? I gave them the brains to do it, and they're killing each other.' He's stuck.

In spite of the Goonish heresies, I think he was very near the truth. It seems to me that the key to this is that God's *only* power is love-in-the-form-of-grace – not coercion, not the threat of hell-fire, not tinkering with the laws of Nature; and that love is easily rejected. Accepted, it is unconquerable. But the essence of the human condition, as the Christian faith interprets it, is that while we cannot escape God's love (it is offered freely and unconditionally to everyone) we are also free to refuse to respond to it. God, then, is *trying* to be active in every second of history, and in every glimpse and gesture of Nature. But most of the time man frustrates Him. God, maddeningly, refuses to hit back; carries on loving.

I think that what I have said here should be common ground to the great majority of Christian churches. Catholics would probably want to go further and speak of grace as having to be *mediated* to us through *sacramental* acts – a sacrament being a visible sign of an invisible reality. Thus a famine relief campaign or a peace march could be a sacrament. I find a great deal of power in this, since it is an old Quaker cliché that the whole of life is sacramental; so the more things become sacraments, the merrier. But some Protestants will be suspicious of this, not wanting to create idols or to grant middle-man status to anyone or anything that might come between the believer and God. Faith is what counts, they say; we want nothing to do with theories which handle revelation as if it were objective knowledge, and then begin posing as compulsory laws. The Catholic Church itself has been through various phases, now stressing the objectivity of revelation, now its subjectivity, now its natural and rational character, now its supernatural and faithful. I think it is fair to say that both sides have broadened their understanding to the point that what matters most is simply keeping up with God's will, not trying to nail it down.

If God is active in history through the response of men, that brings us inevitably to the controversial issue of the Church and politics, where I found less controversy than you might suppose. David Isitt, Canon of Bristol, who pointed out that the prophets of the Old Testament were political figures from start to finish; and could hardly have been otherwise, since the Jewish church and the Jewish nation were always identical. Jesus had inherited that tradition, and to that extent His gospel was a political gospel.

I pointed out that times had changed and that politics were a good deal more perishable than religion. Could we really extract a political message for today from the Bible?

Isitt thought we could. There were some political truths, to do with justice and compassion, that were not perishable. The Bible would not tell you the right thing to do in every situation, but for those who were concerned with doing the right thing rather than simply believing the right thing, he was sure it had something to say.

Bishop Lesslie Newbigin of the United Reformed Church wondered how the heresy had arisen that politics and economics were withdrawn from the sovereignty of Christ, to become a kind of 'liberated area' outside God's control? It was, he thought, a very modern notion. For most of history it had been taken for granted that economics were part of ethics, a fundamental part of how we behaved. The answer, he supposed, was that the aberration had arisen out of the fundamentally pagan concept of man that had taken over since the Enlightenment of the eighteenth century.

'Amen!' cried Donald Soper, the socialist Methodist:

I can't see any future for a church that in God's world doesn't accept that it must be involved in that part of it which is political and economic. A church which claims that the world is for Christ must be up to its neck in politics. I don't say *party* politics – that is more complex. But very often, when people say, 'Let's keep the Church out of politics', they mean 'Let's keep it out of left-wing politics.'

Lord Soper himself pays no attention to them. He believes that the kind of socialism he finds in the Sermon on the Mount is the structure most likely to encourage people to be good. On the other hand:

Capitalism is an evil thing, because it is based on what is called enlightened self-interest, and that is a baptismal name for selfishness. Poverty is a crime. The Church has been very specific on other matters. It hasn't hesitated to speak arbitrarily on the most intimate affairs like sex. I don't see why it should restrict its particularity to those and not extend them to the world of the unemployed.

Bishop Newbigin agreed that the ideology of capitalism was incompatible with the gospel, but thought the mixture of private enterprise and public control was something to be settled on pragmatic grounds.

That particular discussion included Cardinal Hume and the Archbishop of Canterbury, Dr Robert Runcie, who were a good deal less specific. Said Dr Runcie:

I don't think the Church can just blandly say: of course we must have a political attitude on this and that. I've always thought that in the past fifty years we have somewhat distorted the tradition of the clergy emphasising the principles while the lay people dealt with the practical edge of things. Recently we've had the situation of the laymen saying, 'For God's sake give us some nourishment for our problems', and the clergy desperately and sometimes trendily trying to solve what are really problems for the laity.

Cardinal Hume observed:

The issue of Church involvement in politics hinges on the fact that *we* are concerned with people as politics are concerned with people; and you can't divide people up into secular and religious. Whenever the poor are afflicted, or whenever human dignity and freedom is not respected, then the Church has a duty to sound a prophetic note; and it must be prepared to be unpopular on matters which concern politicians as well.

Father Harry Williams had two points to make about politics. The first was: 'No society can be run on the basis that its members are saints. Any state has to take into account that it has to govern sinners, which means there are going to be tensions between one group and another – but it's better to work that out than have bloody revolution.' His other point was: 'No, I would not say at all that the profit motive was entirely selfish and unChristian. A man very often wants to make money so as to provide well for his wife and children. Of course any system can be abused. You've only got to look at the Soviet Union.'

Up on Merseyside the main denominations, led by Archbishop Worlock of the Romans and Bishop David Sheppard of the Anglicans, intervene constantly to stop factories being closed and to bring jobs to the unemployed, though they do their best to avoid marching under party banners. They withheld their support from the 1981 March for Jobs so long as it was advertised as a march to bring down the government.

I found the same attitude on Clydeside where Father James McShane says:

I feel we are here to complement the political parties and knock their heads together occasionally. I think the ministry of Christ is basically reconciliation, and there are times when we can't afford party politics. Our movement is political, but it's non-party-political. We want to get rid of this Red Clydeside image and present the image of a reasonable community trying to work together. If man is made in God's image, he's got to share in God's creative power – not just for his own benefit, but for the benefit of all mankind and for the glory of God. He's got to develop his talents or he's not fully human. Now if he's unemployed, what are we going to do about this? He's going to become not an image but a caricature of God.

James Whyte, Professor of Practical Theology at St Andrews, saw nothing wrong when a moderator of the Kirk Assembly gave a sermon denouncing monetarism as a sin against God – and was told by a government spokesman that his business was the salvation of souls. He observed:

They said that to the prophets of Israel. I think you have to beware of jumping in where you've no expertise; but there's no such thing as a value-free social science, and those who produce economic theories often show they have a certain view of Man. I think the moderator was right to object to the assumptions behind this one – though actually he was talking about a society rather than a government; a society that values money above human beings. That seemed to me a very important thing for a Christian to say at this time.

The Church, then, trying to respond to the love of God by expressing its love for people; and thus showing forth God's love in action and prophecy.

But there is one further way in which many people believe they come to know the mysterious mover, and that is through the arts.

This always troubles me; because although I have had some of my most sublime intuitions of reality listening to Beethoven or Sibelius, it occurs to me that while music may be *about* God, one should realise it is *not* God. Much the same might be said about the Bible. But the Bible has a good deal more authentication as divinely inspired than, say, the late quartets. And what about people who don't like Beethoven? Who prefer Wagner, or Mantovani, or the Sex Pistols? Harry Williams even told me:

I find God very much now in the songs of Noel Coward: 'I'll Follow My Secret Heart', 'Some Day I'll Find You'. They can certainly be applied to some sort of mystical quest. Which I don't regard as separate from human quests. People may sing them with Coward's original meaning and still find their fulfilment, and God, in human love.

Which may be an answer to my concern about the potential snobbishness of seeking God in only the *best* music, but it still leaves me uncomfortable; for it would be very odd if people with good taste were closer to God than the vulgar.

And yet people try to reassure me. Dean Tony Bridge of Guildford says: 'I don't think, in the arts or religion, you can get around the statement, "Those with ears to hear, let them hear. Those with eyes to see, let them see." ' Was he saying that a Mass by Byrd had a higher spiritual value than a country gospel service in some Smoky Mountain chapel? 'I think I *would* say that. Moody and Sankey hymns can move people deeply in the right direction; but it doesn't mean they are as profound as Byrd or Palestrina. I hope that's fair without being snobby.'

I suppose it is a question of distinguishing between the love of God and our response to it – which can take the form of music. Fortunately there are other forms of private revelation available. As St Paul has it, there are varieties of gifts. Some of my interview victims confessed that their knowledge of God's presence had come to them through their parents and their church upbringing. It had never occurred to them to doubt it.

Stuart Miller, a Scots Baptist and religious broadcaster, said with devastating frankness:

I regularly and repeatedly find the whole notion of God quite incomprehensible. Faith, I always believe, takes us to where the language bends and I'm jumping for analogy and metaphor. But in worship, in private meditation and in service, yes I do get a sense of the transcendent and the holy, a presence that is more than the universe and yet personal and benevolent towards me – I'm not sure if I know the meaning of the word love, but there's a very strong benevolence there. And I think at that level I know God.

It often seemed to me in my interviewing that the humbler people were, the more likely they were to be blessed with a direct knowing of God, and that this was particularly true of the women. I remember Ros Manktelow, saying of Jesus:

I find Him somebody I can talk to. It sounds a bit silly, perhaps, but every morning I say to Him, 'Good morning, God, I'm here.' And sometimes, in my more doubting moments, 'Well, *I'm* here.' I do talk to Him constantly during the day, though I don't pray at all. I have these conversations. And I am seduced by music. There are times when I feel this great presence of God in music. It just comes over me at any odd time. I think my whole life is a process of conversion.

I remember, too, Christine Parkin, a Salvationist, telling me how she had prayed at the bedside of her eczema-tormented child: 'Lord, this is yours. You've got to deal with this; it's beyond me and everyone else. I give you John and his need, and I ask you to solve it.' The eczema started getting better from that day. 'We still have to live with the problem, but now I know it's not only mine, it's God's. And I do believe that God is in the midst of us, in our pain and misery. And if He's there, we've got everything, haven't we?'

CHAPTER FOUR
Guilt-edged Religion

If you had asked me at the age of ten what Christianity was about, I would have been quite certain it was sin. Sin was an adult word for being naughty, or in my prep-school language, 'Getting a black . . .'

I knew from experience that it was almost impossible to avoid getting black marks. One forgot music lessons, left one's gas-mask in the dormitory, was caught talking after lights out. The inevitability of this was rubbed in at chapel every Sunday: 'We have left undone those things which we ought to have done; And we have done those things which we ought not to have done; And there is no health in us. But Thou, O Lord, have mercy upon us, miserable offenders . . .'

Sin kept cropping up in prayers, sermons and hymns: 'O loving wisdom of our God, when all was sin and shame . . . Be of sin the double cure. . . To cry for vengeance sin doth never cease . . .' I gathered that in some mysterious way it was my sin, my naughtiness, that had nailed that agonised figure to its wooden cross over the altar. I must, for His sake as well as mine, make every effort to avoid naughtiness; and I tried to some effect, eventually achieving an almost black-free record. But it was really no good, because chapel went on telling me I was a miserable offender and that deep down inside I must know that there was no health in me.

Matters were really more complex than that, but I do not want to weary the reader with my infantile autobiography. To cut the story short, I was faced, from the age of about fifteen onwards, with glimpses into the abyss of depression. For long periods these would depart from me; but each time they came back worse than ever, with the growing certainty that eventually 'they' (the police? the Furies? God's avenging angels?) would find out and that death would be the only penalty for my unnamable secret crimes. This dread grew throughout my twenties, thirties and forties, intensified by my experiences as a foreign correspondent on the battlefields of Vietnam, in the ghetto riots of America, and at the assassinations of the Kennedy brothers and Martin Luther King. At the heart of it, I suppose, lay the recognition that the violence of the world was calling to the suppressed violence within myself. Christian faith offered no help whatever. When I looked at the Cross, with its suffering victim, its only message to me was: 'You did this – and there is no health in you!'

Years later, when I described it over the air, I received a torrent of letters confirming that this is an all-too-common experience among Christian depressives. Jack Dominian, the psychiatrist, analyses it precisely:

What happens is that the quality of depression deepens our sense of unworthiness, our sense of badness and isolation. We interpret this as a distancing from God, instead of a sheer human need that wants God more than ever. We find it very difficult to register love, and because of our culture we think it is our fault. In fact it is nothing of the sort. What is happening is that the sense of our own goodness and value diminishes, and what we need is constant encouragement and affirmation of our value at a time when we have great difficulty in experiencing it.

If I ever had anything like a Damascus Road conversion experience, it came to me on the psychiatrist's couch: for that was where I learnt to recognise the missing element of forgiveness. I emerged from it, and remain today, with a fairly low level of personal guilt and relatively little interest in the matter of sin – which, when I began this pilgrimage, I still felt was over-emphasised by the churches. I asked Dr Dominian whether guilt was something unhealthy?

No, he thought. On the contrary, it was an essential warning signal not to separate oneself from the source of love. Without it we would not be able to reconcile ourselves to each other or to God. The problem was that guilt had become related to being a completely bad person; our total value disappeared beneath it.

Both Catholics and Protestants have given us this view, and it is totally unChristian. You *never* lose the love of God, you never lose the love of your parents. Temporarily you are out of touch with one another, and guilt is the warning of that. It should do nothing to your basic goodness or to your self-esteem.

It looked as though the Church had failed to communicate God's forgiveness to such as me, I observed. Jack Dominian assented:

The Church has done something that is seriously wrong. It has confused this signal of God's continuous love for us with making a person feel totally bad and unworthy. Nowhere in the Bible is there the message that sin alienates man completely from God. But Christianity has failed abysmally to help people realise that when they feel guilty they do not have to reject themselves totally as bad.

What Dr Dominian had to say about the role of the Cross in all this, I shall report in our next chapter. But already I had this assurance – which rang very true to me – that the impression of sinfulness that many of us have gained from our churchgoing is destructive and wrong. The Church may plead that it never really meant what we thought it meant, but it is a bit late in the day to say that now. Where did things go wrong? If, as Hans Küng says, being a Christian is being truly human, then what is the true teaching of the faith about human sinfulness? If we do not get that integrated into the whole, then the whole is liable to be undermined as it was for me.

Alison Adcock, an Oxfordshire Licensed Reader, told me:

I think that the Church is much too keen on sin. I certainly don't believe in original sin. And the orthodox sort of Calvinist position is absolutely shocking and horrible. It's outrageous. But there is certainly something wrong with the human race and probably the whole universe. Somehow or other, fear and greed have corrupted us.

None other of the world's great religions is so closely occupied with the question of sin; nor indeed has the same idea of it. This, I think, goes back to the very person of Jesus who, as presented to us in the Greek-filtered gospels, emphasises not just *what* we do but *why* we do it, our innermost motives. As many would say, we are justified before God not by our works, but by our faith. The right act for the wrong reason is not good enough. This is a very high demand because, speaking for myself, I often find it hard to be sure why I am doing something. Being human, my motives are usually mixed – a confusion of idealism and self-interest. I might help someone across the road because that accorded with my idea of myself as a Christian: but would that be love? Might it not be pride? The most basic forms of Hinduism would see little point in making such distinctions: follow the rules, carry out your prescribed duties, and you can't do better than that.

Judaism finds itself baffled by what Christianity has extracted from its Jewish sources. Stuart Blanch asserts that original sin is not an Hebraic concept, and my two rabbis agree. Lionel Blue says:

Jews don't think in terms of Sin – they break it up into little sins, which you deal with in particular ways. If you've stolen something, you give it back; you pay compound interest on it; and if you can't find the person, you give it to the poor. Whereas with Christianity, sin is like dealing with the entire atmosphere.

Rabbi Hugo Gryn adds:

The sinner in Judaism is never the lost soul, and the repentant sinner is never an abject figure, he's called a 'master of repentance'. Once a year we focus on this, on our Day of Atonement – a twenty-four hour period of fasting, prayer and meditation. The whole aim is to correct our perspective. Now the Christian notion is very different from this, because it is only by divine grace that the sinner can come right. In Judaism the sinner must right himself, and this must be a fundamental difference.

It must indeed. In fact it represents the parting of the ways at a most ancient heresy: that of the fourth-century British monk Pelagius, who thought that man must be personally responsible for his own good deeds and that grace was not necessary for salvation. It seems to me that the ways do not part as drastically as might appear: for while the orthodox

Christian may be *aware* of grace (because of his knowledge of Christ) even the unorthodox and non-Christian still has grace flowing through him, and responds to it whether he realises that or not. But I dare say I have committed yet another heresy.

I have already used the term 'original sin' without pausing to give it a definition. In a crude sense it does go back to the first – the original – sin of Adam. Of his own free will he deliberately disobeyed God's orders, with the consequences of suffering and death which have been transmitted to all his descendants. God had intended that we be permanently bathed and protected by his love or grace, but our ancestor – only enacting what we know perfectly well we all would have done – chose to ignore that love. So we are all born not merely imitating the sins we see around us, but with a very tattered suit of grace that can only be repaired by Christ (or so says the Church).

I must say that at this point I have a good deal of sympathy with Jewish protests at the way Christians tend to push the New Testament back into the Old and give meanings to the Old it was never meant to have. By themselves, the first three chapters of Genesis convey to me a rather different message.

There is Eve, bored stiff with nothing to do while Adam is out naming the animals. Along comes the serpent and urges her to stand up and be a woman – do a spot of thinking on her own account. Why should she be a dimwit all her life? So she and Adam eat the forbidden fruit of the know-ledge of good and evil, and take the consequences. Sex and work are invented for them as a kind of punishment (something on which Christian society has been hung up ever since). But only as a consequence of this disobedience does mankind venture out into the world of choices and embark on such adventures as climbing Mount Everest, sailing the Atlantic singlehanded, writing Shakespeare's sonnets and building the Taj Mahal.

Looked at in this, perhaps not entirely reverent, light there is a certain inevitability about it all. The Lord God knows perfectly well what He is doing, and what is going to happen.

Only *He* is not going to *make* it happen; because at the root of his loving fatherhood lies the gift of free will (and if we do not believe in that, we do not believe in ourselves). You might say that humanity was endowed with free will the moment God gave Adam the choice of naming the animals.

A mere puppet Adam would not have been worth having, and certainly not worth being. Just as someone suspended in silence and darkness in a tank of warm water becomes mentally annihilated, because there is nothing to push against, so an Adam incapable of choosing anything but the best would have suffered moral annihilation. We need evil, we need sin, we need disobedience to push against. So the serpent (also created by God) performed a valuable function, as did Eve. They ought to be among our heroes. And God, having made us with free will, must be prepared to take the consequences – as indeed He did in the Crucifixion.

That, at any rate, is my reading of the Genesis story, though not, I admit, a very orthodox one. For it does seem to imply a certain unfairness on the part of the Lord God, in chucking us out of Paradise for doing what was bound to happen. Stuart Blanch thinks it is not so unfair if you look at the story as telling us not so much about God as about ourselves, and not about the mythical past of the race but about its future.

The author of Genesis, the Archbishop believes, is thinking about the history of his race, its shame and its frustration at being kept away from that Tree of Life by the sword that turns in every direction.

For him, the object of human life is to experience his God walking in the Garden in the cool of the evening, drawing upon its riches and resources with no struggle for existence, with war banished. And he sees that as the end of a long-term process which began with the Revelation to Abraham. So the writer of Genesis is looking forward to a future of the human race based not upon mythological or imaginary past events, but upon certain ideas about relationship with God which he sees as the whole purpose of the Revelation.

As for 'original sin', Archbishop Blanch finds that:

an unhelpful way of expressing the truth ab...
tion. Very often I think it owes little to the b...
practice of infant baptism. Why do you have to...
the waters of baptism? Why, because there must be...
ing to it by the mere fact of its birth. Then what ab...
baptism? Why did He have to have it? If you reg... a
symbolic entrance to the covenant people of God – whic... ot John
the Baptist clearly did – then you don't have to account for this in
terms of Original Sin.

Nevertheless, the Archbishop is not claiming we are all essentially sinless, or that God reproaches us unfairly for what is only the exercise of our free will. 'A responsible person knows that he has to make serious choices. But he also knows that very often they are wrong choices or choices that go bad.'

John Bowker, theologian of science, prefers to talk of *ab*-original sin; meaning not the particular faults we commit but the fact that we are conditioned by our genetic codes and by the immense histories that have gone before us, things not of our choice or determination but which determine us.

The important thing to grasp is that while we are born in a determined condition, we do have the freedom to acquire insight, maturity, responsibility to make something of the materials entrusted to us. That's where redemption as new freedom leads us into the communion of saints, where we realise our full stature.

History, our heritage, plus our own disinclination to alter things, have produced a kind of built-in tribal sin which up-to-date thinkers tend to describe as 'structural'. Neville Black, a working-class Merseyside vicar, told me:

I can see the government and the church as *demonic* institutions in which sin is structured. Or let me take a more difficult example: Oxford and Cambridge are great symbols of British education, liberating for some but at the same time denying many more than they liberate. A sin isn't just me in my one-ness; it's me trapped within the many-ness of prejudice, the wilful denial of others so that I may live. That's the problem with the inner city. We have allowed it to become impoverished so that the suburbs may live.

ecclesiastics about sin, you keep being told that
its Hebrew origins the word means 'missing the mark,
falling short, failing to measure up to your highest standards'. At first this sounds like a bit of hard luck; but the
Church insists it is more wilful than that. It is less like sport
and more like a business transaction. There is, in Genesis,
an implied contract between God and Adam, which Adam
breaches; just as there is an explicit one between God and
Noah. And the framework of contract, covenant or treaty
between God and Israel becomes stronger than ever in Exo-
dus, Leviticus and Deuteronomy. In the Old Testament, sin
becomes a violation of the contractual relationship between
God and man, where man substitutes his own one-sided
interests for God's will on our behalf. And it is important to
recognise that as God's covenant is with, and His will is for,
His people, so the individual is required to serve not merely
his invisible God but his visible neighbour among that
people. To betray that neighbour is to betray God. Loving
one's neighbour as oneself was an Old Testament commandment long before it was re-issued and underlined in the New.

Sin, therefore, was tending to become a contractual issue,
something to be defined and regulated in the small type of
the religious life; and that is one of the things Jesus was
protesting against. It was not enough, to Him, that one
avoided extortion and adultery, fasted twice in the week and
gave tithes of all that one possessed. What mattered was that
one should honestly confess oneself a sinner and cast oneself
upon God's mercy – admitting that one's own efforts were
not enough.

And yet this still left unanswered the question of what was
a sin? Jews had known clearly enough, because it had been
codified for them. But Christians were in a new situation.
Dietary and other Jewish regulations did not apply to them.
They were told there was a New Covenant.

Early in the history of the Church it was recognised, sen-
sibly, that there were degrees of sin. A prime consideration
was to avoid scandal to the Church, so that apostasy,
publicly-known adultery, murder, were high on the list. As
the centuries went by the catalogue of sins that had to be

confessed was expanded and a tariff of penances introduced. The connection between the two led to an almost magical belief in the effectiveness of confession, penance, indulgences (a relatively late invention of the Church) and extreme unction in securing the admission of the soul to Heaven. The distinction also hardened between grave or mortal sins and less serious or venial ones. But where *was* the distinction exactly? One of my favourite mediaeval theologians is Johannes Major, who argued that to steal from one to five ears of corn from a rich man was no sin at all; to steal from six to ten ears was venial; but to steal eleven ears or more was mortal. Later moralists would say, I think, that mortal sin is a conscious rejection of God which alienates us from Him, whereas venial sin is that temporary hiccup which we repent and which can never separate us from God.

Mediaeval Catholics found themselves blindly confessing the most trivial of sins, believing that man was incapable of changing for the better, save for grace received through baptism and a life of repentance. The reformers were hardly more optimistic. The point about Calvin, however, is not that he wanted to make every sin a mortal one – though he did believe that all sinners deserved death and eternal damnation for their disobedience to God – but that he reacted against Catholic casuistry by asserting that if sins were pardoned by God, it was solely through His mercy and nothing to do with their triviality. The battle of justification by works or by faith was joined, the reformers arguing that turning to God in faith was what mattered, with repentance as a thank-offering and good works as the fruit; and the counter-reformers arguing that even the most faithful could have his justification diminished by sin or increased by works. The Pilgrim Fathers of North America sought to comfort themselves in the presence of their wrathful deity by arguing that their material success was a sure sign of His forgiveness and their election to grace.

The memories linger on, not only among prosperous American evangelists but among such liberated Catholics as Spike Milligan:

I felt all the time, sin, sin, sin – thinking about women or playing with myself, reviling all my natural instincts, which was wrong. Jesus is not going to send you directly to Hell for that. I needed some help, but I guess the Church doesn't know that – it suppresses you, lock, stock and barrel, and it's very sad. Except, I met a Jesuit priest in Rangoon at St Paul High School, and I was desperate. My mother and father, being Catholics, wouldn't talk about sex at all and I was starting to notice pretty girls. I said to this priest: 'Do you think about women?' And he said: 'All the time. All the time,' he said. Irish. It worked like shattered glass: it was a wonderful release for me.

I have been in trouble myself, accused of antinomianism (a kind of religious anarchism) for suggesting that Jesus himself actually preferred the company of sinners to that of the righteous. Certainly he was not regarded as respectable by the pious establishment of His day, and I do not get the impression of a man who consorted with 'publicans and sinners' simply for the purpose of lecturing them about their sins. Michael Taylor, a somewhat unorthodox Baptist, looked dubiously at the notion of Jesus as the perfect human life; for 'He was clearly limited, and – as far as I'm concerned – incomplete as a person. He had much to learn. But we don't necessarily confuse that with being wrong in a disturbing sense.'

Professor Charles Handy, who works in what might be described as a religious think-tank in Windsor Castle, is one of those who believes that not only was Jesus capable of sin but that he probably did sin.

Sin, in a way, is God's gift to man. If you have the power of choice, you will sometimes choose wrong and you will sin – the wrong choice is so often more tempting, and so it was for Jesus, for goodness sake! He needed to pray desperately to God who was in Him, who was Him, so that He did not make the wrong choice. But even if He had made the wrong choice – that doesn't matter, provided that you make the right choice sometimes, even just once, and that shows up not in your life so much as in the life of others, particularly of those who come after you.

I don't think Cardinal Hume would have subscribed to that. But I found him sympathetic to my own personal unease at feeling more aware of God's forgiveness than I felt bugged by the menace of sin. 'If it ought to bug *you*,' he observed, picking up the Americanism, 'It ought to bug me even more.' He went on:

But my faith has grown strong in the love and mercy of God. The two classes of people who are my particular friends in the gospels are the crooks and the crocks – it astonishes me, the numbers of them there are; and that's the human condition. So, in a sense, our weakness and our sinfulness are our greatest claims on the mercy of God. Rather like you, I'm not over-anxious about my frailty. There are more lovely things to dwell upon.

But we still do not seem to have made much progress with helpful, practical definitions of sin.

Metropolitan Anthony of the Russian Orthodox Church in Britain has a characteristically mystical idea of it. Sin, he thinks, should never be defined in terms of behaving badly or behaving well – that is a distraction. Sin is something much more interesting. For it begins with our refusal to live deeply with all our being – which to me sounds very like refusing to have any religious life, or to recognise the religious dimension in everyday life.

It is easy to live superficially and never to take the risk of diving into the depths and facing the terrors of the deep. The result is, living superficially, we are unable to reach out to God – because God is deep.

And at the same time we prove unable to reach out to our neighbour; because our neighbour can only meet us in the depths. On the surface he can only conflict with us. Apart from that, of course, sin means our lack of integrity – it means going against our knowledge of what is objectively right and wrong.

Quakers have a saying 'The *silence* brings Unity', and I found this image of unity in the silent depths, unity with God and unity with my fellow human being, an image of great power. It clearly belonged with much that I had been hearing about alienation and reconciliation.

Bishop John V. Taylor of Winchester has another, converging approach.

I think sin is anything which leads to a greater deadening of one's mind, one's personality, one's feelings. God is ultimately interested in my being totally alive: everything that comes from Him is life-giving. I think that my belief in the Devil – call him what you like – sees him as the personification of the inbuilt false promise that goes with a great many experiences – they hold out false hopes of greater vitality. We think: if I do that, I'll get a kick out of it. Well, each time you get less and less of a kick, and it ends up making you deader instead of more alive. Whatever we do that creates deadness is a sin. And in terms of society, if I organise some institution the end result of which is the greater deadening of the human community, then that is a gigantic sin.

I wondered about the invention of television . . .

John Habgood saw sin as:

the dark reflection of the special abilities which man has been given by God. In man's very freedom there is the possibility that it might be used in ways that are destructive. I see the whole peril and pain of creation as being precisely to create that which can respond freely to a reality which otherwise could so easily dominate it.

The psychologist Jung's idea of the 'dark side' of our personality has been most influential; and several of my victims were tempted by psychological theory. Stuart Miller, the Scots broadcaster, said he would be much happier with a picture of the human mind in which there was no inherently evil element – only 'personality distortions'.

I mean, lust is simply love that has become overstretched, violence is physical force overstretched, selfishness is a very legitimate self-interest overstretched. It would be awful if we lived for each other all the time. Every force within the human personality is legitimate, but it ought to be held in a certain tension, a certain equilibrium. But we have, to use the traditional language, 'fallen'; we are distorted, out of equilibrium. The virtues within us are very often minimised. I like to think of my Christian faith as an attempt to bring me back into an equilibrium where all these different forces are being exercised to the extent God meant them to be.

Stuart, I think, just escaped on to the side of the angels by subscribing to the view that to be truly human is to recognise God's will for us.

Father Harry Williams uses the word 'integration' instead of 'equilibrium', and brings in Metropolitan Anthony's depths.

We are a collection of selves, aren't we? The more superficial levels not being agents of the deepest self, where God is, but flying off on tangents of their own. That's where I understand sin. There is the self I put on for the benefit of other people, the self I put on for my own benefit, the self I hide away in a dark cupboard because it's wounded and damaged and ugly and I don't want to see it. Ultimately I believe all these selves will be integrated and woven together under the inspiration of the final or deepest self which is God.

Which is very moving, but there is a mysterious paradox here of which we have to be aware. People are telling us to be faithful to our true self: but that self *is someone else* – it is God within us, not just hooray-for-good-old-us. John Stott, I think, would be very suspicious of too much emphasis on this 'God is inside me' approach. Stott says:

Sin is very serious because it is the assertion of myself against God my creator, against His love and authority and against my fellow human beings. It's me first and my neighbour next (when it suits my convenience, which isn't very often) and God somewhere in the distant background.

I found a disinclination on the part of even the most progressive theologians – Dennis Nineham, for example – to play down the seriousness of sin. There was even a tendency to look beyond it to a positive power of evil, as distinct from an absence of good. Kenneth Barnes, the Quaker educationist, admitted that there had been a time when he considered that:

Sin was very overdone, because consciousness of sin can be a terribly inhibiting thing, especially in churches where there is no provision for the sort of confession there is in the Catholic church. That was wicked and destructive – it destroyed more people's lives than we can count.

Nevertheless, thought Barnes, when you looked at the tortures, murders, hijacks and kidnappings in the world to-day, evil was a very real thing. Quakers tended to let 'this business of God in every man' blind them to the reality of the enemy.

I'm very much of a Jungian, and I feel Jung's concept of the dark side in all of us very near the truth. If we equate that dark side with the Devil, we are not far wrong in our understanding of what the Devil is up to.

The interesting thing about the dark side, or the Devil, is that he was a fallen angel – he belongs to God really – and our problem is to reconcile the dark side and make use of its energy. It's always recognised that the Devil is walking up and down the earth, full of energy. In education I used to find the apparently wicked boy was full of it. You've got to understand it, come to terms with it and make use of it. In other words, bring the Devil back into God's Kingdom.

David Watson, the evangelist, believes fervently in a transcendent power of evil: 'I have seen the manifestations of demonic power in the lives of individuals which would make it very hard for me to deny the existence of evil as an intelligent force.' And Paul Oestreicher, a very different breed of Anglican, says:

I really believe in this great cosmic battle between good and evil of which the Book of Revelation speaks. When you have, as I have, grown up first of all with the personal suffering of my own family, the death of some of them in the Nazi concentration camps, and then gone on living while other people suffer, it's hard not to want to strike back. And yet this is the great Christian contribution: that the vicious circle has got to be broken, and it can only be done with love.

Well, that will be the point of our next chapter. In the meantime we have allowed a rather terrifying picture of evil, complete with Devil, to build up. But there are some very ancient philosophical problems about the Devil which have been recognised all through Christian history. For example Origen, the third-century theologian, was clear that if the Devil *was* a person, then he could be redeemed by Christ and we ought to pray for him. And if we take St Augustine's fifth-century view of evil as the absence of good, then the Devil, being absolute evil, cannot exist. It seems to me that the Devil is an extract of the corporate *us*.

We, of course, are individuals. But as modern Christian thought rightly emphasises, God and religion concern themselves not just with individuals but with community; and modern community sciences tend to analyse breakdowns in terms of frustration, deprivation, alienation and disadvantagement rather than of sin. Thus they miss either a transcendant source of goodness, or taking evil seriously.

David Jenkins of Leeds is a practical theologian who says he is trying hard to bring back a realism about sin, 'and to attack both the optimism of alienation language and the pessimism of people who say that nothing works. I think if we were more realistic about evil we could be much more hopeful about the way things go wrong.'

Jenkins admits he is *almost* getting back to believing in the Devil, but won't because of the principle 'No entities beyond necessity' (which I take to mean: don't invent characters you don't need). Things, however,

do build up in such a way that they get a momentum of their own which seems to go totally perversely in an evil direction. So that you almost feel you need exorcism. A prime example was Nazism. Part of the problem is that sin is indefinable. But if I had to say quickly, I would say it is the *nonsensical* power which takes people over and to which people contribute; whereby they go against that which is best and hopeful and human. It is destructive for the sake of being destructive.

It seemed to me that Canon Jenkins was saying sin was, in the end, irrational. And yes, he was.

I think one of the alarming things you have to face up to is that

73

there are good and bad things that do not fit together. The world does not cohere. It shows manifestations of heavenly goodness and hellish badness – for which I have a word, and that is sin.

The word 'nonsensical' was intriguing. God, it seemed to tell me, knows what is best for us; but allows us the liberty of saying we know better. Which is nonsense. But freedom is not freedom unless it goes as far as permitting nonsense, the freedom to assert our independence by choosing something we cannot in fact control but which takes us over. And so we arrive at a helplessness which makes us cry out for help – a cry which God is waiting to answer.

It all seemed a long way from the Garden of Eden, where Eve had nothing to do all day but make up her mind whether to go bathing in the Pison, the Gihon, the Hiddekel or the Euphrates. I thought of the Quaker George Fox and his amazing vision of being 'Come up in the spirit into the Paradise of God, where I knew nothing but pureness and innocency and righteousness, so that I was come up into the state Adam was in before he fell . . .' I could not presume to have been that far, though I met a Salvationist who had his moments of total grace. Temperamentally, though, I was unable to share the awareness of malevolent evil that some of my witnesses knew. Perhaps it had something to do with my own sense of forgiveness. Where did that come from? Did it come from the Cross? To this, with apprehension, I now turn.

CHAPTER FIVE
Jesus Saves – or Does He?

It's not the Fathers of the Church who made British Christianity what it is; it's the hymn-books. Still trudging along at the back of my head is a compound dirge that goes something like:

> *When I survey the wondrous cross*
> *Without a city wall,*
> *My richest gain I count but loss:*
> *He died to save us all.*
>
> *He died that we might be forgiven*
> *When all was sin and shame.*
> *Love so amazing, so divine,*
> *To the rescue came.*

The melancholy of the music and the impenetrability of the words convinced me, in my boyhood, that here was something which – like the mysteries of sex – might be explained in adulthood but would be considered in bad taste for a child to question. So I went on singing. And it never was explained. Many years later, in my twenties, I wrote to the English Presbyterian who ministered at my London church and asked if *he* could explain from the pulpit. How had Christ saved me by dying two thousand years ago – and from what? Why was being executed for annoying the Romans a gesture of love towards me? And having read a little light theology, I wanted to know the distinctions between Sacrifice, Redemption, Atonement and Salvation, please. Was the Crucifixion one of them or all of them? There seemed to be differences of opinion on the subject.

The minister was a good shepherd to his sheep and very properly declined to alarm them by putting on an intellectual fireworks display for the benefit of one young Oxford undergraduate. He lent me another book, laying out all the rival theories of what had really been happening on the cross. I gathered that the earliest traceable theory had been that Jesus, by dying, had somehow conquered the hordes of evil spirits that had been plaguing men; but that after a century or two the more legal-minded Latins had converted this into a transaction with the Devil, a ransome paid for the release of souls from Hell. Beyond that lay a succession of satisfaction theories, penal theories, ethical satisfaction theories, moral influence theories, mystical theories, social theories and psychological theories. The Roman Catholic Church, I gathered, was particularly emphatic that explanations that made the action of Christ merely exemplary or inspiring, or some kind of divine disruption of the natural order, were out. Otherwise you paid your theologian and you took your choice.

And yet there was no denying the central and irresistible power of the Cross. It was the single feature upon which all the churches were agreed. It had inspired the most burning of devotional literature, the most eloquent of painting, the most moving of music. What was more, millions upon millions of simple (and complex) Christians had pinned their faith to it and had not been disappointed. Christianity was Crosstianity. It was literally crucial.

I have already outlined something of my own, home-made Christianity before I began this pilgrimage: how, in particular, I had seen Jesus as a supreme example of non-violent resistance to evil. It also seemed to me that Jesus had deliberately courted death: 'He actually willed this upon himself,' agreed Spike Milligan, and then argued against calling it suicide by drawing a controversial parallel with the IRA hunger-striker, Bobby Sands. My own theory was that, frustrated by his disciples' insistence on clinging to his earthly coat-tails, Jesus had in effect told them that unless he departed physically, they would never find the Christ in themselves.

Cardinal Hume said that made a lot of sense to him. 'If they were to get beyond just the man whom they saw and with whom they lived, He had to leave them so that they could understand what He was. It is the gift of the Spirit to bring that understanding.' I was a little disappointed not to have been nourishing a heresy; but although I might have contributed one small brush-stroke to the scene around the Cross, it was clearly not the whole, rich picture.

Incidentally, while one layer of my instincts told me to follow the reformers, reducers and simplifiers, another was responding happily to the appeal of this richness. Why should there be only one correct answer to the mysteries of faith? Did not the power-points lie at those very places where several different answers, coming from different directions, crossed; with the Cross itself the most complex of them?

If the point of the Crucifixion had been simply Jesus' departure, He could have chosen other, less painful ways to go. It so happened that I had done a certain amount of reading (nowadays known as 'research') on the subject of crucifixion; and I knew that far from being the equivalent of hanging or beheading it was, in fact, the most ugly, humiliating and agonising method of execution known to the ancient world. Peculiarly abhorrent to the Jews, cursed by their scriptures, it was applied by the Romans particularly to slaves and subject peoples of whom it was intended to make an example. It was preceded by a brutal flogging after which the victim was compelled to drag his own cross to the place of execution where he was literally tortured to death. Quite apart from the agony of the nails, his body was arranged in such a way that he could neither alleviate his pain nor hasten his end, which could take days. Jesus, in a sense, was lucky to die within hours. The spectacle was so horrific, so humiliating, that Cicero called it repulsive, St Paul a disgrace, Origen utterly vile; and the early Christians could not bring themselves to use the Cross as a visual symbol at all. The nearest we have come to it in our own historic times has been the butchery of hanging, drawing and quartering. We would do well to think of crucifixion in that context, rather than as some dainty tableau by Raphael.

In an age when idealistic trouble-makers are still being tortured to death as a deterrent, the significance of the form of Jesus' own death should be obvious. Whether he was God or man or both, things have not changed. He suffered what we suffer, and we are still doing what they did almost two thousand years ago: and yet perhaps I should not have introduced the modern political prisoner into the picture, because it implies a certain nobility, and my argument here is that to Christ's contemporaries there was nothing noble about crucifixion at all. Half the point of the Resurrection is that people saw it as defeating not just death but the very worst sort of ultimate dehumanisation that the world could devise. To triumph over that, they argued, He must have been more than human.

And yet the doctrine of the Cross says more than that. It tells not just of the glorification of Jesus, but of our redemption, atonement, salvation. To quote the doctrinal statement agreed by the joint Anglican and Roman Catholic International Commission: 'Through the life, death and resurrection of Jesus Christ, God has reconciled men to Himself . . .' and again, 'Christ's death on the Cross was the one perfect and sufficient sacrifice for the sins of the world . . .' There are at least two ideas here: that God and humanity were alienated until the death of Jesus somehow bridged the gap; and that the sins of mankind somehow demanded a sacrifice, an offering on God's altar.

Once again, Stuart Miller – like many another honest believer I know – is:

Absolutely baffled. I cannot accept that the death of Christ was a traditional Jewish sacrifice, because that was always a thank offering. The only kind of 'substitution sacrifice' was a goat – and we never hear about the Goat of God, so the Lamb of God thing absolutely mystifies me. If we say that Jesus died for me – well, I know fine well I die, so He can't have. On the other hand, I am reluctant to go to the other position and say that it was an expression of great love, because if it wasn't a sacrifice of some kind, then He simply got himself killed and that wasn't love, it was simply defeat. It was a demonstration of tolerance, weakness, that kind of thing, but not love. So I'm stuck. I'm baffled.

Father Harry Williams has no difficulty in accepting that:

Jesus on the Cross showed us that the highest value which human beings can articulate is self-giving love to the death. But I don't see any metaphysical transaction with God which somehow changes our status towards Him. It seems to me the status of human beings with God must be the same before and after Jesus. I can't believe that something happened in AD 33 which changed God's attitude towards us. I've read most of the books about the Atonement and I can't see any which have much meaning for me.

Father Williams is not the least bit worried that he is setting himself up against centuries of teaching by the Church. But I must say *I* am still worried how Christ can be seen as dying *for* us, or even for his disciples. It is not as if His death got them off a criminal charge. If we must look beyond a mere example (and most of the churches insist there is more than that) then surely there *has* to be some metaphysical effect.

Not only laymen like Stuart Miller are baffled by the problem. One of England's most celebrated monks confessed to me: 'I honestly don't know. It's one of the things I really must sit down one day and try to work out. At this stage I just accept it. But don't for Heaven's sake broadcast that!' So I didn't.

Dennis Nineham insisted that he regarded the Cross as more than just a jolly decent example to us all: it had opened up the possibility of a relationship with God which would not have been possible without it, and we should be grateful that was so. But the professor was suspicious of:

efforts to probe behind the supernatural scene and work out a sort of heavenly mechanics. I don't think the limits of the human mind allow us to penetrate like that. I know people tried in earlier times, but I think we have learned to be more conscious of our limitations. I would say God is secret to Himself.

Which was curiously like some of the more old-fashioned interviewees. George Reindorp, recently retired as Bishop of Salisbury, remarked of my question as to how Christ could die for our sins:

This is the hardest thing for people to realise intellectually. You can tell them about it, but I believe the experience of Christ's death, the freedom from sin, can only be experienced personally. You can hear about it and know about it, but I think this is the gap across which a person has to leap by experience or by faith.

John Stott, the evangelical, pointed out that Jesus' death did not, in fact, save us unless we availed ourselves of it by faith. He went on:

It's a horrible idea to think of Christ as a third person saving us from an angry God. But I believe that God *in* Christ came into the world, identified himself with our sin and guilt and bore the consequences of that in the death He died. Now we are approaching the ultimate mystery of the Atonement; and I keep together two affirmations of Paul. One is that God actually made Christ to *be* sin for us. The other, that God was in Christ reconciling the world unto Himself. How God can have been in Christ when He made Christ to be sin for us, I don't know. But I have to keep the two together or I will go sadly wrong.

Sadly, I am afraid, I had to move on from that paradox. I like paradoxes; I think they are ideal for some theological purposes. But that one did not work for me. What on earth could have St Paul meant by Christ *being* sin? Surely the Church did not admit that Christ was sinful? And if it meant that Christ picked up and 'bore our sins' there was an element of unfairness, impossibility, that I for one found hard to take.

This came up in conversation with another Anglican bishop, John B. Taylor of St Albans (not to be confused with the other Bishop Taylor, at Winchester).

Bishop Taylor *had* sat down and thought it out. Yes, he said, Jesus died for the sins of the world. What happened at Calvary was a demonstration of God's love, but it was more. It was a way in which God showed the awful consequences of sin – a link with the Old Testament system of sacrifice. Within the metaphor of the sacrificial lamb lay the idea that because of the sins I had committed, my life merited nothing but destruction from a God of any justice at all. Without the redeeming love of Christ, my life was forfeit. 'But He takes my place and dies for me.'

That, I thought, postulated a rather vengeful and blood-thirsty God, who had to be placated by sacrifice.

'No,' said Bishop Taylor.

The idea of having to be satisfied is an emotional, human term. But justice demands punishment, and clearly if I stick my tongue out at God and live in disobedience to Him, God would not be just if He did not say, 'You have cut yourself off from Me, and you must suffer the consequences. But, recognising that you have sinned, I will come to meet you more than half-way. I will be the father to the prodigal son. I will come to greet you, because I still love you. You have still done wrong, but I will help to effect the reconciliation.' And that is what Christ has done for us on the Cross.

I still did not see how, and protested, 'But they are our sins – not His. We still commit them, and we still get punished.'

'No,' said the bishop. 'We do not still get punished.'

'We still take the consequences of our sins, surely?'

'Only in the sense of the normal human consequences – but they are very, very minor. The total consequences of sin have been taken away. The judgement of God upon us has been relieved and we are forgiven. We still fall short, but we don't have to go in for self-flagellation. He picks us up and we can go on with a clear conscience, because there is the famous verse: "The blood of Jesus Christ goes on cleansing us from all sin." '

It seemed to me the 'normal consequences' of sin were far from minor. I knew that it was possible to experience God's forgiveness; but was it really necessary to believe certain things about the death of Jesus for that to be effective?

I don't think you have to adhere to a particular theory of the atonement. Our hearts and our minds sometimes respond very differently. But for myself, what Christ did on the Cross triggers off a response of immense indebtedness, of great relief that the punishment I know is my due has been borne by Christ and I can be relieved of it.

It occurred to me that the burden which, for the bishop, had been relieved by Christ, for me had been relieved by a Central European psychiatrist. Not that I thought my psychiatrist was God. On the contrary, he had lifted the veil cutting me off from God. He had been the mediator. Was it possible – if rather shocking to the pious – to think of re-demption like a successful course of psychotherapy? The bishop was hardly the one to put that to, so I tried it on Jack Dominian. He liked it. Psychotherapy was helping human wholeness towards the divine integrity. Salvation was by-passing the psychological detail and reaching directly to God by exposing one's being to God's mercy.

Then was the Atonement a kind of divine psychotherapy on a cosmic scale?

That is not going too far. I keep on saying Our Lord was the first psychiatrist, with a penetrating awareness of human beings ten times better than psychological theory. And finally, what He did on the Cross was to take all the human ingredients and transform them into both a human wholeness and a divine wholeness. Only Christ could achieve that.

What Our Lord could do was to take the fulness of being divine and transform it in terms which we could understand. He could, on the Cross, express His fear of being abandoned with the certainty that He was not. None of us, as human beings, has that hundred-per-cent certainty of the divine presence. It was only God that could have this awareness of the Father.

By that argument, Jesus had to be God; and I still could not see my way to saying that was flatly so. But one morning, as I was coming home from my daily contemplative stroll, I found myself saying: 'If Jesus was not God, He is now.' I cannot believe, any more than Harry Williams and Dennis Nineham, that Jesus intended His followers to say, 'You are the second person of the Trinity and the Holy Ghost begot You.' Nor do I think he was totally immune to sin. What I do now believe is that over the ages the company of His followers – the 'communion of saints' that I trust – has come to see God almost exclusively through Him; has come to say, 'God is like this. God is so like this that as far as we can ever tell, God is this – for we are not likely to come any closer.' Into the figure of Jesus, the saints have poured all that they know of God.

Is this a subjective Christ – something for which the Church would never stand? In a sense, I suppose it is. But it is a collective subjectivity, not the construction of the individual (though the faithful Christian will always make his own contribution to it). To claim to know the objectivity of God – God as He is without us – seems to me presumptuous and impossible. People like Nineham are entirely right to say, 'It all depends what you mean by Divine.'

Atonement is at-one-ment. What Dr Dominian was telling me was that the wholeness of being human could only come through reconciliation with God, who was the essential ingredient in true humanity. But why did Jesus have to die on the cross to achieve that? I could accept that time had to be left out of the equation: if we were dealing with something on the scale of God, it did not much matter whether Christ had existed in the first century or since all eternity, or whether he died before or after our sins were committed for His actions to have their effect on them. But why His death? I could see that Bishop Taylor's belief in sacrifice and divine justice was shared by many Christians – and to that extent was part of the 'collective subjectivity' – but no light lit up on the panel of my own conscience.

Lord Ramsey, jovial ex-Archbishop of Canterbury, had another go from the same general direction:

It's rather hard to explain this combination of the condemnation of sin and an act of divine compassion. Never, never must we say that Jesus died to appease an angry and hostile God – it all proceeds from God's love. God was in Christ reconciling Himself to the world. But His doing so involved a *cost*; because the forgiveness of sin isn't just an easy-going matter, as if to say, 'Well, you sinned, but it doesn't matter all that much – I forgive you.'

I tried the evangelicals. Michael Green of Oxford argued:

What died in Adam and Eve when they ate the apple was that intimate, unspoiled relationship they'd had with God. And when the Bible says Christ died in our place for us on the Cross, what it is saying is that the Lord Himself has dealt with that alienation and has undertaken all the guilt and responsibility for it. I think this is really the heart of what happened on Calvary: that it was an elixir of life to a part of our being that was dead.

David Watson of York told me:

We have broken God's commandments again and again, and in the court of God's presence we are manifestly guilty. I believe it is only because Jesus actually took our sin and God's righteous judgment upon Himself that we are saved.

Watson's associate, Graham Cray, took it further:

I have been forgiven for that for which I do not deserve to be forgiven; and yet somebody has paid the penalty – that almost directly substitutionary idea has got to be part of the picture. But this is also an act of almost universal reconciliation, which every individual may choose to accept or not. And it is as though the whole of the evil of the world was focused in God the Son. Part of the biblical picture is of a great battle between good and evil.

If that was so, I remarked, what a waste! The world was as wicked as ever, wasn't it?

Graham Cray affirmed his belief in the Second Coming and the Day of Judgment. But that was only half the story.

The other half is that when individuals *do* respond to what Christ has done for them, you simply can't continue to sin. You know at once you have had this encounter with Jesus, and it is morally life-transforming.

The Salvationists could quote example after example of that; the kind of testimony that makes the sophisticated titter, but which one knows does happen to those most in need of it. Michael Green cried: 'Jesus is alive! He's doing things all over the world! It's true, it's relevant! Here in Oxford I've seen over two hundred people come from communism, atheism, agnosticism and nominal Christianity to Christ since last October. And that's only in *our* church.'

But what about those of us – me, for example – who cannot pretend we are either poor or poor in spirit: how are we to inherit the Kingdom? If alarm over sin does not make us push open the door, should we, perhaps, return to the physical spectacle of the Cross and take up that feature of it which screams in our faces – its suffering?

That was something which fascinated and bothered my

Jewish friends. 'There's so much mystery in Christianity,' complained Lionel Blue.

For example, that Jesus' death pays the bill for your life. At that point I think most Jews retire exhausted from the fray. At the same time, of course, we are aware that life is a mystery. There are enormous problems and great mysteries for us in the Holocaust. How many prayers must have been said in those cattle-trucks that were never answered! Was all that suffering in vain? How does God use it? Christianity offers a bit of an answer – which shouldn't make the whole answer – namely, that suffering is redemptive, that it's really a good in disguise. I don't think any Jew can swallow that. Suffering did make a few people very great. But it brutalised very many; it made them animals.

Coming from a Jew, I think we have to take that very seriously. But as one of my Catholic priests, Father James McShane, pointed out, Isaiah's figure of the suffering servant, who atones for the sins of others, is one of the high points of the Old Testament.

I think the New Testament writers saw this fulfilled in Christ, and that's why they present Him in the language of the suffering servant, of the innocent who takes upon Himself the sufferings of us all. That's why it's the most quoted passage in the New Testament.

And this is true: that to greater and lesser degrees, we all suffer, whether we think our sins have merited it or not. Perhaps if we forget about our sins for the moment (cries of 'never!' from the Calvinist right) we can press forward a little.

Una Kroll, who is a doctor as well as a deaconess, is all too familiar with suffering – including the suffering caused by people's religious tangles over sin.

And I experience Christ's suffering so much in other people, the ugliness of death and dying. But in a mysterious way I expect to find sacrifice and death valuable; people can wrest value from it. It depends very much on your concept of the world and of God. But if you do believe, as I do, that any action of love and sacrifice can build up love, then even in the face of the horrific forces of evil that exist, the only worthwhile thing is the sacrificial love that can redeem. Nothing else can withstand evil except the power of love. Vicarious suffering – suffering for others – is such a difficult thing to talk about, but I've seen it so often: a mother longing to suffer for her child – although I know it's ridiculous to say that her suffering can benefit her child or anyone else's, yet in some mysterious way – like Christ's suffering for me – I believe that it is redemptive.

Where had I heard talk like that before? I remembered. It was from Martin Luther King, just a few days before he was assassinated. This very readiness to suffer, to absorb evil, to offer oneself as a soft target that would divert it away from others and allow it to burn itself out and sterilise itself was profoundly moving and somewhere at the heart of the moral order.

'I am like this – I am so like this that as far as you are concerned I am this.'

Up in Scotland, Bishop Michael Hare Duke had told me:

I believe that the first thing about the Cross is that it is a declaration of the way God is: not an attitude of 'Down on your knees you rotten little sinner', nor an attitude of 'Back to your hutches while I sort it out': but a statement that God is vulnerable. If that is so, my whole attitude must change, because if God is vulnerable, then I have got to be vulnerable and live that way.

Now this is not simply a story to which you say, 'Cor, ain't He luvverly?' – you've actually got to do something about it. There is something in me that story can hook into. Something happens like an exchange of current. It's a story that saves – a very powerful act of God to change. But when it comes to 'There was no other good enough to pay the price of sin' – that's not on.

Ivor Smith-Cameron said:

I know that whenever I hear about Christ as Saviour it appears that He saves us from sin – and I don't wish to deny that – but in my own experience He more than does that: He releases from *fear*, and I think fear is the great killer. It is the opposite of faith, trust or commitment to God. All of us are paralysed by fear of our own unworthiness, fear of the sense of guilt, fear of being judged, fear of fear itself. When I think of Christ as my Saviour, personally I think of Him more as He who releases from fear.

Very well, then: Jesus who shows us there is nothing to fear in being vulnerable like God, like Him; and who shows us by suffering. Suffering that is the consequence of our sin, be it wilful or 'aboriginal'. But I would speak now of a Christ who, rather than being made to be sin for us, was made to be suffering for us.

Maurice Wiles helped to put it in the context of eternity:

I think the traditional accounts of Atonement and Redemption have tended to start with an assumption about the Creation and Fall. They see Creation as something that was perfect at the beginning, which men then spoiled with their sins, and which at some point in history had to be restored to proper relationship by something dramatic. Now seeing the Creation and Fall as a story (I'll avoid the word myth), I believe in Creation as something continuous that is going on all the time. So I see Redemption as something that is going on all the time, as the fundamental character of God's creative activity. And I see the Cross as focusing this truth of God's reconciling love working for the harmony of His Creation.

Wiles moved me on to face another important truth: that no Christian *can* think of the Crucifixion without the Resurrection.

Crucifixion seems to me to show that the way this reconciliation may be achieved is by breaking the continual process of revenge. And Resurrection expresses the confidence that this is the way the world is ultimately built. It is a long-term process, and it does not do away with the fact that very often this is the way of disaster for those who practise it. But it does express the conviction that in the long run this is the only way in which human violence and self-destruction can be overcome.

Peter Cornwell of Oxford added a further dimension. We must not forget that the Jesus who appeared was also the Jesus who disappeared: the Resurrection was no triumphalist display of the glory of Christ.

I think the key thing about it is that the love which had been poured out on to that small parcel of land in Palestine – a love which always seems to have been champing at the restriction – was liberated to be available to all men in all places and all times.

In a long and thoughtful meditation, John V. Taylor of Winchester drew the threads together for me. He saw Jesus as going to His death believing that somehow it was going to prove God's way of inaugurating the Kingdom; and hoping that some of His disciples would go through it with Him as a collective act. When He realised they would not:

This quite awful thing happened; when the God he had trusted so implicitly suddenly was not there. He was totally let down by a God that had moved off. And then, it seems, that moment of desolation was followed by a kind of willed commitment – Father, into Thy hands – whereby you could almost say, here is a man recreating God. He is absent; but into those absent hands I will fling myself – and God must be there.

He suffered. He went through that darkness which must be the very depths of what so many people in depression go through. And then something convinced His followers, who must have been absolutely broken by the event, that He was still alive. I can't believe that this tragic desolation was suddenly turned into brightness and light by a kind of 'John Brown's soul goes marching on' – I think it was more than that.

Once His followers have got to that point, their minds go back to this extraordinary intimacy with God which they have seen in Jesus. And they reach the point where they say: whatever is true of God, we have seen it in this man. There is a link between this man and God that is closer than anything we have ever known.

So they start looking at God from the point of view of that experience, and reach the conclusion that somehow His suffering on the cross, His going through that darkness, is not only His entering into the universal experience of the worst – so that He is one with man – it is also saying something about God. It brings God into this suffering. So that from that moment there begins to dawn this extraordinary idea that God Himself is in all the desolation, has had to bear it, and that He is the underlying suffering – that deep-rooted pain in the universe from which love grows.

That deep-rooted pain: the pain of separation from the loved one, the pain of love ignored, the pain of love literally crucified.

There was a coda to this waiting for me in Chester, where

William Vanstone is one of the canons, author of a book I have long admired called *Love's Endeavour – Love's Expense*. Its theme is that love – including the love of God – which is not recognised, received and returned is love tragic and uncompleted. William Vanstone illustrated it like this:

I once had a parcel through the post, containing a lump of cheese. There was no sign where it had come from, so I put it into the larder – and it was very good cheese, too. Months later I wanted a piece of paper, and when I smoothed out the wrappings from this parcel, I found a little note tucked away, saying it was from my niece who had been on a school visit to a cheese factory. She had bought a piece of cheese with her own money and sent it to me with her love. Now, if I hadn't found the note, I would still have got the cheese; but I would never have known what it meant – which was far better. I wouldn't have got the love.

Those with ears to hear, let them hear.

CHAPTER SIX
One-way System

It's a scandal: to be precise, the scandal of particularity. In the gospel of Matthew, Jesus asks His disciples: 'Whom say ye that I am?', and in that of John, He answers Himself: 'I am the way, the truth and the life: no man cometh unto the Father, but by me.'

It's a scandal in the Greek and Latin sense of a stumbling-block or obstacle. Why should God have chosen this particular man in this particular place and time? For it seems not merely unfair that Christians should claim an advantage denied to those unlucky enough to have been born Hindus or Moslems, but unlikely that God would have been so contemptuous of the latter. Multitudes of millions were born and dead long before Jesus appeared in Palestine; and, notwithstanding the best efforts of Christian missionaries, multitudes more since then have had no real chance either to accept Christ or reject Him. Is it not arrogant, and racist, too, to claim that Christianity is in some way a superior faith to the others – that there is only 'one way', the Christian way, to salvation? True, there are biblical texts supporting the view that we are all children of the One God, that there are others 'not of this fold', and that Israel at least will be saved because of God's faithfulness to His covenant with her. But for centuries the official Christian line has been, 'No salvation outside the Church'.

That line is weaker today, if only because the definition of what the Church is has widened. Some would say it includes all who strive to do God's will. But there are still people like Dr Raymond Brown, the Baptist principal of Spurgeon's College, who says: 'I believe Christ is unique as God's Son, and that God had no other way of revealing His love.'

No other way? Wasn't that rather tough on the Moslems, Hindus and the rest?

Well, I think it is, and I don't say it in any arrogant or dismissive sense. I wouldn't want them to compromise the light as they understand it. There can be great moments of insight in other faiths. But when Christ said 'No man cometh to the Father but by me', I want to take that absolutely literally.

Stuart Blanch, too, accepts that saying at its face value. Even if you have reservations about whether St John's gospel reports the very words of Jesus, the Archbishop thinks there is no doubt the saying represents what early Christians believed, and that that therefore it is a reliable reflection of what Our Lord taught His disciples.

Of course it does seem very harsh. But from my own point of view, I know no other saviour. As a young man I've paddled about in Buddhism and various other philosophies; they were helpful to me and I don't regret any of them. But my own experience is that only in Christ do I really find the truth, undiluted and uncompromised. Whatever value I attach to other religions, from my point of view they are ancillary – not an alternative to revelation in Christ.

Archbishop Blanch went on to give the basic reason for his confidence in Jesus' saying and in the whole Christian religion:

I don't have doubts about the intellectual truth of it, because I've had to teach it, so I have had to work these things through and be exposed to the most radical criticism of it that is possible. I've had to face all the questions not only in my own mind, but in other people's minds as well. Of course, that isn't the whole of the matter, because a man may be intellectually convinced and yet have the most serious doubts about his own standing, his own problems. Nevertheless, however I may feel, I can still say to myself: never mind, it's true just the same!

Well, true for the Archbishop, maybe. But what about the Moslem, for whom the way of Islam is equally true – and just as exclusive? This worries me, because some five years of my life as a foreign correspondent were passed in India, Pakistan and the Middle East; and although I never felt tempted to change my religion, I could not then and do not now find it in my conscience to deny that my Hindu, Moslem, Buddhist and Sikh friends were 'coming to the Father', and in many cases were closer to Him than I was.

The experience of India was particularly impressive for me. At first sight, it is an appalling society, riddled with poverty, disease, injustice, superstition and apathy. The caste system makes Britain's class system look positively enlightened. And yet, in a clumsy way, it works. The intolerable becomes tolerable, the unmanageable is somehow managed, the nonsense makes sense to those who are part of it. I always get accused of callousness when I say this, but there is about life in India a purpose, stability and even gaiety that to a Westerner is almost incomprehensible. If one can only still one's natural impatience and sit quietly watching India go by, one begins to realise how the poor may, indeed, be blessed, how the meek shall inherit the earth, and the pure in heart see God. I used to get my clearest inklings of this sitting by the banks of the Ganges, watching Bengali villagers taking their ritual morning baths and making libations to a sacred peepul tree. It was little different from watching Italian peasants crossing themselves with holy water, or Athenian typists lighting a hasty candle before the ikons on their way to work. I could not believe that God had not always been on the banks of the Ganges, long before Christian missionaries arrived there: and I have met Christian missionaries who agreed with me.

But this is not to say, carelessly, that one religion is as good as another – what can 'good' possibly mean? – or that everything in Christianity can be found in Hinduism. Hinduism, in any case, is an entire culture, a way of life. In the religious sense, it is not a single dogmatic faith but a loose federation of beliefs and practices, ranging from abstract mysticism to anointing phallic symbols with butter. In some parts of India, Christianity is accepted as just another member of the loose federation, and Jesus as one of many incarnations of the godhead. There is a strong sense in most Asian religions that man is born to pursue conscientiously the fate laid down for him; so that it is unnatural and blasphemous to pit one's will against destiny by switching to a different faith, especially one that is alien to the culture and liable to disrupt the order of life. Conversion – seen by the churches for centuries as a divine command – is regarded by most Asians as an outrage. Gandhi, who had many Christian friends and referred constantly to Christian hymns and scriptures, strongly disapproved of it.

Old-fashioned bible-pushing proselytism is out of fashion these days, sometimes because it is banned by governments, sometimes because the churches themselves have come to see it as rude, often because missionaries feel that service and education are a better way of spreading the Kingdom. Dean Horace Dammers, who spent four years with the Church of South India, returned grateful for what he had learned from his Hindu and Moslem friends. But he did emphasise the liberating effect that conversion had upon the poorest of the poor – those not even admitted to the lowest rank of the caste system. It reminded me of how Metropolitan Anthony had responded, when I complained to him that two thousand years of Christianity had left us as bad as we ever were:

I don't think we are as bad as we were. There is a great deal that has changed since Christ brought into the world a quite new notion of the value of the human person. In the ancient world there were masters and slaves, like owners and cattle, and no common measure between the two. Christianity has brought the notion that every single human being has an absolute value. The life and death of God-become-man shows you how God values man.

Nevertheless, in my own experience the Indian untouchable who becomes a Christian often has to pay a heavy price for his liberation. For once he starts demanding his rights as an individual, the caste structure descends on him like a ton of bricks.

In many ways, however, Christianity is an ideal faith for the newly literate. It offers hope to the aspiring individual, its scriptures are easily accessible (though they have hidden depths), and the same may be said of its basic theology. Its central figure, Jesus, is one whose real existence and history appeals to the Third World. Even so, it is not an overnight business to root out fatalistic and superstitious religion and replace it with something more sophisticated. John Harriott, the Roman Catholic writer and broadcaster, thinks Christianity is almost unique in rejecting fatalism and pushing responsibility back upon man.

I think it is terribly important not to think of God as the first agent in everything. Either you say 'I don't want anything to do with Him because He's doing nasty things to me', or you think 'He's doing all the kind things and I don't have to bother'. The cumulative effect is to increase human irresponsibility. Whereas I think Christianity is entirely about making people responsible for themselves. No – man can't save himself, I agree, and there are lots of ways in which we are not free agents. But I think Christianity presents the free agency of man more definitely than most religions or forms of magic do.

There was a time when the Church would hardly admit that other religions looked towards the same Creator God at all. That is not so today. Bishop Taylor of St Albans has no hesitation in saying that in their various faiths all people are worshipping the One God, and indeed have received revelations of Him through obedience to those faiths.

One must therefore have a profound respect for them and recognise as co-religionists those who have tried to be obedient to the heavenly vision. I would far rather my brother Moslem remain faithful to his observance and his prayer than that he fall victim to our secularising society.

But that respect leads me to recognise that if the Moslem is true to his faith, he is equally convinced of the ultimacy of Islam. It isn't only Christianity that claims this uniqueness. In Hinduism there is this rather dismal conviction that the whole thing is illusory and it's just the great unknown having a game with us, which I find hard to feel sympathetic towards. But we have to start this dialogue between faiths respecting in each other the inability to give up the belief that our truth is the greater. I think that's inherent in religious experience. If we start from there we can still go on to loving each other instead of fighting each other, and I think something new may come. I don't know what it will be; we have hardly begun.

I tossed out to John Stott the rather woolly popular view

that all faiths were much the same and we would all arrive in Heaven together. Stott pounced. Only the ignorant could say all religions were the same: it simply wasn't true. Hinduism and Buddhism taught that I must pay the penalty of my own sin if not in this life then in the next, or the one after, in an endless cycle of reincarnations. But that was the antithesis of Christianity. Christianity was not earning your salvation by human merit. It was the undeserved forgiveness of God offered to us because Christ died for us, and you could not reconcile the two approaches. Islam, too, was a religion of human merit, and the symbol of the Koran was the scales in which Allah balanced your merits and demerits. But the symbol of Christianity was not the scales but the Cross – the work of Christ, not our own good works. 'Christianity', pronounced John Stott, 'is unique. It is peerless.'

Ivor Smith-Cameron, who comes from India himself, was far more ready to grant other faiths equal status.

I think that God is one, and I have deep respect for people of other faiths who respond to God as their communities have done down the ages. The Christian community has, through much of its missionary endeavour, failed to take seriously the spiritual journeys of others. In doing so it has lost out on its own fullness. In calling Himself The Way, Christ points beyond the Christian community to the deep truth the spiritual pilgrimage has for all faiths and times. Those of us who are brothers and sisters know that in talking of Jesus as the way, we are at one with other people who are on their journeys. He is not only the way, He is our guide along the way, He is the goal of our way. Christian unity itself is only part of a deeper unity of people of all faiths, and that is only part of a deeper unity of all mankind.

Canon Colin James has stood in the bazaar in Old Delhi, surrounded by thousands of Moslems, and thought to himself:

These people will never hear of Christ in my lifetime. What has God been doing in them all these centuries? Is God absent from them? I must recognise God at work in their laughter, in their love, in their coming to terms with their sufferings, in their prayers.

Travel suddenly opens the windows of the soul to the reality of God in other people. If the humble Hindu on the Ganges can't be saved unless he becomes C. of E. or Baptist or R.C., then God is not the God *I* want to believe in. Your faith depends literally on where you stand. If you stand in France you are a Catholic. If you stand in Burma you are a Buddhist. If most of the people in Ulster who are vehemently Protestant had been born in the south, they would have been Roman Catholics.

It seems to me that at this point there are two points worth summing up: first, that it is outrageous to look down on non-Christians for being as they were born; and second, that it is wrong to say all faiths are the same. But various arguments bring pressure upon these points.

If non-Christians themselves are not to blame for their condition, perhaps Christians are to blame for not having converted them? Two further arguments arise. Proselytism is not necessarily wrong – I have met Indian tribal people and Fijians who argued convincingly that the missionaries had rescued them from a degrading barbarism – but proselytism has too often been arrogant and destructive. And Christianity might have made more progress if it had shown its virtue in works rather than words, particularly in the behaviour of allegedly Christian nations. Further, if God has revealed himself to all peoples, and since their conditions vary, who are we to say that *our* understanding of Him is more appropriate to India than Hinduism?

But then, again, that might be an argument for deploring the birth of Christianity at all, for saying that Judaism and paganism should have been left as they were, unchallenged. Human understanding of the truth is not static; there is movement and, if you will, progress which has to break through at some specific place, some specific time, through some specific person, even if it does seem 'unfair' to people out of reach of them. Jack Dominian argues that Christianity is, in fact, one of the 'fairest' of religions, since it draws upon at least three surrounding traditions: the mystical religions of the East, the down-to-earth pragmatism of Judaism, and the absolute ideals of Greek philosophy. 'Hence, wherever

Christianity goes, it is able to reflect something local because it has so much richness in its own ingredients.'

Dr Andrew Ross, of the Church of Scotland, illustrated this as he spoke about Christianity in Africa:

It is an insult to Africans to think that Christianity was ever imposed upon them. On the whole, colonial governments didn't like African Christians because they were taught to feel themselves equals. But on top of that, in almost every part of Africa I know, Christianity spread because Africans spread it. Take the Xhosa in South Africa, who have produced all the nationalist leaders like Steve Biko: they chose Christianity and interwove it with their own traditions to produce what really is a Xhosa Christianity – not a twisted or perverted Christianity, though. Often the African Church got down to the roots of what it was about almost instinctively, because what the missionaries did was to give out the Bible in the indigenous language.

Now when a village African read the Bible, he found in it a world he could understand. He went straight to the Palestine of Jesus' day, and it smelt and sounded like his own world. African people, I think, often get closer to the spirit of the Bible than Western readers do.

So Christianity, by this argument, has not merely a truth that can speak to many conditions, but an adaptability. But that can be in more than one direction. Andrew Ross cited also the example of Afrikaner Dutch Reformed Christianity:

The people who left the Cape in the 1830s in the Great Trek and founded the Orange Free State, they went away without any ministers of the church at all. But they read the Bible every day, and as they went through this experience of the Trek and of founding a new land for themselves, they developed a popular religion out of their own experience. It's a very Old Testament religion – the African is identified with the Amalekite – and although it formally nods its head to Calvin, it has left Calvin far behind. For example, they talk about the Afrikaner people as being elect. Now Calvin was quite clear that individuals are elect to salvation; but it's quite impossible that Calvin said nations were elect. Nationalist ideology grew out of that kind of folk religion, developed without theologians or contact with any other intellectual world. It's very strange – uniquely Southern African.

So there are dangers in Christianity going it alone in a strange land. Michael Hare Duke quotes another Japanese Christian dictum: We are dealing with a God who has a crucified mind, not a crusading mind.

That is to say, He is not out to bash all the others. We have got, I think, to take the other religions enormously seriously, asking the question how much of the crusading, jungle mentality is in them and how much has God, in those faiths, broken through to the crucial truth that somehow you win by losing. Where we, as Christians, have done the crusading thing, we have actually betrayed Christ; because that is not His way at all. We have got to find the spirit of God in other world religions, make our contact with the positive things in them, and not tell them to forget the lot and start again.

At the Regent's Park mosque in London, Gai Eaton – a great ecumenist among world faiths, as well as being a spokesman for Islam in Britain – argued that you could find in Islam not merely elements of every other great religion but even the essence of them. (Moslems accept that Jesus was 'a divine messenger' and that his sayings were authentic revelations. They argue, however, that drastic alterations were made to the gospels and that Christians are misguided in failing to recognise, in Mohammed, the perfection of God's word.) Speaking personally, Gai Eaton told me:

I believe that the religious are separated providentially. As the Koran itself says, if God had wished to make us all one people, He would have done so. I think it has been necessary that the divine essence, which in itself is one, should be refracted as in a prism into different colours.

I'm not going to say that misunderstanding is essential, but I think some of them play their part. Religion does not exist to teach us philosophy, it exists to save souls; and I believe that there is, in the divine way of doing things, a very practical element – an awareness that on the whole most people need to believe that their religion is either the only true one or unquestionably the best, if they are to give the whole of themselves to it. And if one tries to persuade people that all religions are true in a rather vague way, they'll end up with someone like Mr Jones of the Jonestown mass suicide.

Gai Eaton finds the thread of unity in what he calls 'the consensus of the mystics of the great religions. To me, there's absolutely no question about the unanimity that is there.' I had to agree with that; though I can't help feeling it is rather like finding a similar uplift in the music of India and Germany, but no agreement between them on how to treat a toothache. Perfect mysticism, I suppose, is total silence; but most of us have more mundane things to do.

Eaton, however, gave me one example of what he considered the ideal attitude towards other religions. Pope Pius XI had once dispatched an emissary to Libya with the words: 'Do not think you are going amongst infidels. Moslems have attained a salvation – the ways of God are many.'

I have left, some pages behind, the point that it is wrong to think all faiths are the same. Deliberately, I did not say they were as good as each other, for that drives past the questions of for whom, for where, and for when? And if we mean as good at getting us into heaven – that is a question on which even the most superior prelates defer to the Almighty. I know there are people who know they are saved. I know many more who expect to sweat it out a bit. I am not much taken with those who know that other people are definitely *not* saved.

David Watson believes very strongly in the uniqueness of Christ. 'There is no other leader that can bring us to God. You cannot find God through Buddha, Mohammed or Confucius. Only Jesus.' But he wrestles with the problem of the 'saved infidel'.

If man has separated himself from God by going his own way, then he needs a bridge to bring him back to the other side. Jesus is that one bridge, bringing God and man together. Now it may be possible for me to cross that bridge without actually knowing that I'd done so. There are people who have responded to God in so far as they understand Him, and have come to a living trust in God through Jesus Christ the Bridge, without actually knowing that the bridge was really there.

I thought that a bit far-fetched, and said so. Watson did not think it was.

There's just one mediator between God and man – the New Testament letters indicate that. But it might be possible for a person actually to cross through Jesus without knowing much about the details. And it seems to me from the teaching of Jesus that judgement is according to the response we make to the opportunities we've had. And ultimately only God Himself knows about that.

Paul Bates gave things a new, if unclerical, look:

If 'I am the way, the truth and the life' means that the Jesus preached by the Church is the only way to salvation, then that doesn't seem to me to figure with what the earthly Jesus was talking about. *He* is actually asking a much more difficult thing of me. He wasn't on about obeying all those rules and regulations. He was saying: keep your eyes open – I am the frame of reference, the glasses to see through: you see things in a very different way. Do you know that quotation from Simone Weil? 'If I appear to stray from the path that leads to Jesus in my search for truth, I will not have gone very far before I meet Him standing there.' That's always meant a great deal to me.

There may be tut-tutting in the cloisters at the suggestion that Jesus could be met standing *outside* the Church; but I must admit I like it. Even though I can see that, just as the atheist might be cross at being told he was really inspired by the Holy Spirit, so the non-Christian might be annoyed to learn he was really wearing Christian spectacles or crossing a bridge called Christ. But if what Jesus meant was not the bleakly exclusive 'I alone am the way . . .' but, more embracingly, 'The way, the truth and the life *are all Me* – everyone who comes to the Father is following that way, that truth and that life that I stand for . . .', then there would seem to be room for me and my Hindu, Moslem, Buddhist and Sikh and Jewish friends to meet one day on the same mountain top. Plus, perhaps, a few Marxists, Humanists and Freudians.

Let me embark on something of a purple passage:

I see God as a vast mountain with its top vanishing into the clouds and its circumference disappearing over the horizon. We do not know what its limits are. Each of us stands in a slightly different position in relation to that mountain; each of us gets a somewhat different view of it. The nearest we – as a human race – can hope to get to a conspectus of the mountain is by adding together our different views, not by pretending (what is impossible) that we can all stand on the same spot: for we were not put on the same spot.

Increasingly we have learned, and we are able, to visit one another's points of view. By doing that we can appreciate why some people say the mountain is green and gentle, others that it is fierce and rocky, others again that it is clad with pine forests. It is all the same mountain, seen from different angles; and to deny any of those points of view is to diminish the true nature of the mountain.

Equally, to endeavour to approach or climb the mountain as if we could tackle all those features simultaneously is to doom ourselves to an ineffectual and possibly disastrous expedition. It is not impossible to move over to a different base-camp, a different route. But fundamentally I believe that each of us has been set an appropriate route to climb and would do best to follow it. (Incidentally, that does not rule out the possibility that some views of the mountain are deceptive and even dangerous.) But we can all witness together to the existence, majesty and glory of the mountain.

Most of us, if we are wise, will follow a guide who speaks our language – though there will always be some who insist they can follow their own lonely way. Some of the routes toward that unseen and here-unknowable summit lie adjacent to one another; some may cross or eventually run together. One party may call across to another, help another out of difficulty, donate some provisions, offer advice on the way ahead. One party may find a harder, steeper and loftier route than another; or again, may settle down to picnic idly on a plateau and cease climbing altogether. Most of our expeditions have been climbing for centuries; the climbers are the great-great-great-grandchildren of men and women who set out long ago. How futile it is to criticise each other for not having arrived on precisely the same path together! We cannot turn back (though some are tempted to). We can only do our best from where we are. But we are still on the same mountain.

End of purple passage.

Hard-line Christians will continue to insist that by seeking to extend the truth I am corrupting it. And yet the last thing that I – or Gai Eaton – want is one vast amorphous world faith, averaged out from half a dozen. People like me may become exasperated at times over the devotion of the faithful to what seem like trivial and irrelevant doctrines, rituals, symbols. But these have power and meaning and richness. They are sacraments (please wait till Chapter 11 . . .). To throw them all into one melting-pot would be to reject the revelations that have come to many worthy communions of saints.

Personally, I think that as a working faith for the modern world the Jewish-Christian tradition is streets ahead of the others; but I have no doubt, either, that some of the traditions of Asia have much to teach us about worship, contemplation, the inner nature of the Godhead; besides affirming that in many ways Christianity is not so far ahead on all fronts as we like to imagine.

However, it seems to me also that other religions are not lightly to be dabbled in, for their own sakes or ours. An enriching religion is not just a philosophy or system of ethics, it is a community. We should not carelessly cut ourselves off from our roots and bury ourselves in a soil for which we are not conditioned.

One of the most appealing figures in Hinduism is that of Krishna, the Voice of God in the Hindu scripture known as the *Bhagavad Gita*. Krishna says of himself: 'I incarnate myself from age to age, to save the righteous, to destroy the wicked, and to re-establish the right way.' It is tempting to see in Krishna (whose name is so like Christ) the Hindu equivalent of Jesus. But this is quite wrong, not only because Krishna's message in the Gita is totally unChristlike, but because far from being a unique and final revelation, Krishna is only one of many incarnations which according to Hinduism have been or are yet to be.

Buddhism, which now enjoys considerable respect among Westerners because of its emphasis on non-violence and contemplation, does not really conceive of a personal God at all. Its concentration upon the suffering of humanity (which it attributes to selfish desires and attachments) chimes with some of the views I have presented as Christian. But the reaching of Buddhism towards *nirvana* – a blissful annihilation of the illusion of selfhood – involves a view of the essential worthlessness of the world which is wholly alien to the Christian notion of a benevolent Creator God. The law of *karma* – an iron law of cause and effect, of endless rebirth which can only be mitigated by individual effort – is equally unChristian. The Buddha himself (a real enough person) claimed only to be a teacher of the way, not a saviour who could bear the sins of the world or effect any metaphysical change in the cosmic system. Michael Green told me the effect that Christianity had had on Buddhist converts of his acquaintance:

They don't say, 'Down with Buddhism! Up with Jesus Christ!' They say: 'That which we have been feeling after, that desire to know and be known, that longing to be forgiven: that sense of a personal relationship, when all that Buddhism offered us was something totally impersonal which did not match up to that personal which is the essence of me – that we have found in Jesus Christ.'

It's not because of aggressive evangelism – though there is plenty of that in Oxford, with which I occasionally have something to do; it is generally because of the lives of Christians living alongside these folks. And it's not often a matter of their abjuring their past, but seeing it come to fulfilment in Jesus.

Green gets converts from Islam, too, and one knows of a handful in the opposite direction, Christians turning Moslem. But although Islam's simplicity and brotherhood is appealing, it will probably be handicapped in the West by its conservatism; both in the form of its insistence on using the Koran in the original Arabic (the Koran cannot, strictly speaking, be translated, only paraphrased) and its refusal to develop or adapt to Western conditions. Islam, again, offers nothing equivalent to Christ's work for man on the Cross. Indeed, while it insists upon the Virgin Birth it denies that the Crucifixion really happened, and it regards it as a serious heresy to present God as having any kind of partner.

So there are major obstacles in the way of any compromise or merger between Christianity and the other great world religions (we have already noted some of its departures from Judaism); though this does not mean they could never influence or modify each other as they have done in the past. Myself, I think India the most likely place in which a major development of Christianity might take place, although nationalist Hindu resistance to the spread of the churches might be severe and even bloody.

We should take seriously Gai Eaton's advice about man's need – or God's providence – of a unique and infallible faith. If a merged world-religion is unlikely, the alternative (as we might see it) of an expanded Christianity would have to come delicately and by example – not by head-on attacks against other faiths. Christians would have to ask themselves constantly, 'Why should other people wish to be like us?' Christians would also have to suffer, and they would have to be clear in their minds what they were suffering for.

In a studio in Broadcasting House, London, Chris Rees and I gathered four representative church leaders: Robert Runcie, Archbishop of Canterbury; Basil Hume, Cardinal Archbishop of Westminster; Lord Soper of the Methodists; and Lesslie Newbigin of the United Reformed. I asked each of them what, at the heart of it, the Christian faith was about.

Said Lord Soper:

It's about the truth of what sort of universe this is, and where I can find the power to do better. Jesus tells me: in penitence and faith and in thinking about Him and endeavouring to serve Him. For me, the heart of Christianity is coming together with other like-minded people, in order that I may be forgiven my sins and find my way to the Kingdom.

Bishop Newbigin answered:

For me the heart of the matter is the fact that God, in the Cross and Resurrection of Christ Jesus, has met and mastered all the powers of sin and death; and has opened a way – which way is Himself, His body and blood – in which I am called to share, and called therefore to be a witness to the whole of creation that this is so: a witness in word and deed.

To Archbishop Runcie, the heart of the matter was:

Keeping alive the spirit of Jesus Christ. It was a spirit which took the negative and destructive things in life – evil, sickness, even death in the end – and so handled them that they increased the total output of goodness in the world. That's what redemption means for me; and it's a spirit that is hopeful, that makes rather hollow-sounding words like 'Kingdom of God' and 'Heaven' *mean* something. So it's a matter of caring and coping with the negative things – and hoping about the future.

All this time, Father Basil had been clasping his hands in agony, as if he were trying to squeeze out the answer between them. At last he said:

For me the heart of the matter is this: it's discovering the meaning of the mystery of God's tremendous love for us all. And having discovered the beginning of what that may mean, to respond to it. And by responding to it, to discover the meaning of the love of our neighbour.

After all, the first commandment is to love the Lord our God with our whole hearts and our whole minds, and our neighbours as ourselves. But that can only happen truly when we begin to realise the love of God for us.

I remembered what a weighty Quaker, George Gorman, had once said to me, in words that had illuminated my heart:

'The truth about life is love. And the truth about love is that it is God.' If that is the way, the truth and the life – if love is the way – I should gladly welcome any fellow pilgrim who treads it.

CHAPTER SEVEN

The Ghost that Came to Dinner

By the age of ten I was perfectly at home with the Holy Spirit; or, as the 1662 Prayer Book taught me to call Him, the Holy Ghost. My prep school headmaster – whose discipline had a lot to do with my oppressive image of God the Father – used to tell ghost stories every Sunday evening, by the light of a guttering candle; my schoolboy magazines were full of them; we used to whisper them hoarsely to one another after lights out in the dorm. The Holy Ghost was clearly a demonic spy, sent to haunt us for our sins and report back to higher authority. He was always about in the quad, while the Father and Son were relaxing in their heavenly studies.

But if the third person of the Trinity was the first to make a direct impression on me, He (or was it It?) was also the first to fade. God was God. Jesus had been a real person. But ghosts (by now I was twelve) did not exist. Further, God the Father was the hero of the Old Testament and God the Son of the New, but God the Holy Spirit had no book of His own; even the references to Him in the gospels and epistles turned out to be vague and shifting. He was likened to water, wind and fire, but there were many passages where there seemed no good reason why He should not be translated into the influence or presence of God the Father or Son. To this day I find some of the most eminent scholars are evasive about Him. Professor C. F. Moule of Cambridge accepts that three-foldness is less vital to the Christian concept of God than 'the eternal twofoldness of Father and Son'. (But of the Trinity as a whole, more in Chapter 8.)

I have to confess that one of my reasons for approaching the subject of the Spirit so dubiously is that I find it the most exploited and abused piece in the Christian armoury. As Hans Küng complains, when theologians do not know how to justify a particular dogma, they appeal to the Holy Spirit.

When fanatics do not know how to authenticate their whims, they invoke the Holy Spirit. The Holy Spirit is called in to the authority of unconvincing statements of faith, and is made a substitute for credibility and objective discussion. I have even heard the Holy Spirit given the credit for successfully whipped votes in the General Synod of the Church of England. An adaptable, and at times mercenary, spirit indeed!

Some writers have identified the Spirit with *Sophia* (Divine Wisdom), which in Greek is feminine; thus seeking to introduce the missing female element into the Godhead. Certainly I found a strong apprehension of the Spirit among my female witnesses. Ros Manktelow spoke of the relentlessness of God. 'He does keep at me,' she said, 'I don't think He's saying anything. I'm just very much aware of His presence. Sometimes I wish He'd go away, but He doesn't.'

Eleanor Barnes, who calls herself a 'Quakolic' because she is a Roman Catholic who also attends her husband's Quaker meeting, thinks the Holy Spirit is the common ground between the two.

And the Spirit obviously has a good laugh over the whole thing, because He's very much apparent in both, although the Catholics don't talk about Him as much as Quakers do. One can feel Him working in both. So often I will come back from mass bubbling either with fury or delight over something that's come out there; and this will be echoed in the theme that is taken up by the meeting, even though the Quakers will say they have no regard for the Church's year or its language; nevertheless the concerns are very much in common.

Quakers would hate to limit the Spirit by attempting to define It. But Mrs Barnes has no such inhibitions.

The academic expression of it would be the love flowing between the Father and the Son, in which we get caught up when we get caught up in God. One keeps going backwards and forwards between the two, and it's the Holy Spirit that does it.

When you feel it operating it is a personal thing. It is a presence more than just an idea or an accident. Just as a person affects one in drawing one out, so that you become more fully yourself and find the other person, so the Holy Spirit does that between people and communities. You see it operating. You see people who don't want to do things – like me not wanting to become a Catholic – suddenly finding that is exactly what they must do. Although it is painful at the time, it's only afterwards that you suddenly see, yes, this was absolutely right.

John V. Taylor, having annoyed the atheists by telling them their everyday experiences are really bumpings into God, goes on to say:

My own attempt to understand the Holy Spirit has convinced me He is active in precisely those experiences that are very common – experiences of recognition, sudden insight, an influx of awareness when you wake up and become alive to something. It may be another person, or a scientific problem, and suddenly the penny drops. Every time a human being cries 'Ah! I see it now!', that's what I mean by the Holy Spirit.

Bishop Taylor continues:

I think if you look into those experiences there is an element in them of something other than yourself that causes that sudden awareness, that waking up. And the man who says, 'Oh, but that's just going on in my brain' is just as likely to be wrong as I am when I say, 'No, it's something independent of you.'

So there is no denying that plenty of Christians believe strongly in the Holy Spirit from their own experience. So far I have quoted some of the more down-to-earth of them, and I must say they impress me. I am somewhat less comfortable in the presence of the more ecstatic devotees of the Spirit, and of those who take off into realms of mystic adoration which have a feminine aroma without the conviction of feminine experience.

But perhaps it is time to go back to the Bible. 'Come Holy Ghost, our souls inspire and lighten with celestial fire . . .'

As I remarked earlier, there is relatively little about the Spirit in the first three gospels; though they do show It descending upon Christ at the baptism by John, and It seems to protect Jesus against the temptations in the wilderness and to give Him His authority to teach and His power to heal. This has given some trouble to theologians because of the implication that Jesus needed to have something *added* with which He had not been equipped before. Others have explained it away as a sign to outside observers of what was already there.

Jesus tells his disciples that the Spirit will instruct them what to say (even before Pentecost); but in these first three gospels He does not make many other references to It. There are the obscure warnings about the sin against the Holy Ghost: in one case this seems to refer to denying the faith under persecution; in the others, to doubting the goodness, authority or divinity of Jesus Himself. Then there is the promise of the comforter, the Paraclete (or advocate), most specifically in the farewell discourses in the gospel of John.

John's is the most controversial of the gospels and I do not feel qualified to take sides in the debate over whether it is the earliest and most authentic or the latest and least. Certainly it has been powerfully influential in the moulding of Christian theology, in which it played its part from an early enough date to be accounted one of the foundations of the faith. In the fourteenth, fifteenth and sixteenth chapters of St John's gospel, Jesus tells His disciples He will ask His Father to send them 'the Spirit of truth, which proceedeth from the Father' and 'He shall testify of Me'. The Spirit, therefore, will not speak independently of Christ, for (to use a newer and clearer translation at this point) 'All He tells you will be taken from what is Mine.' However, Christ makes it clear that the Spirit will be telling them some things they have not heard before: 'I have yet many things to say unto you, but ye cannot bear them now . . . Howbeit, when He, the Spirit of truth, is come, He will guide you into all truth . . .' Jesus adds that the Spirit – the holy advocate – will prove the righteousness of the faith and convict its enemies of wrong.

In spite of its insistence that the Spirit will bring nothing that is not already in Christ's mind, this passage clearly opens the way to developments of the faith beyond what is explicitly in the gospels. It is, in fact, a merciful escape from the faith's becoming fossilised, though it does open the way to prophets leaping to their feet and claiming that the Spirit has advised them Jesus wants us all to become nudists, celibates or vegetarians. Such messages have to be put through the same rigorous tests I described earlier. The openness of Christianity to development and growth has been the kind of blessing and curse that, by maintaining tension within it, keeps an institution alive.

And then came Pentecost, the rushing mighty wind, the tongues of fire, the speaking in strange languages. What really happened? Or, if we cannot be sure of that, what does the story signify? Lord Ramsey, who is the author of a simple, powerful and extremely biblical book on the Holy Spirit, does not believe the disciples miraculously began to speak in different foreign languages – though that is what the book of Acts suggests on the surface. He believes:

They were lifted out of themselves, so that they let themselves go in a burst of ecstatic noises, expressing their deep fellowship with one another and their joy in the Lord. But the emotional, ecstatic part of it was just a symbol of the fact that this great power was going to be within them – not just something of Jesus outside them.

Pentecost, to Lord Ramsey, was the opening of a new chapter, saying: 'This power which you have seen in Jesus is going to be working through you, so that you will be doing great and wonderful things.'

Lord Ramsey takes a view which is borne out by Paul's writings: ecstatic babbling (*glossolalia*) in no identifiable language was a widespread feature of the early churches, and modern Pentecostals and Charismatics have revived it. At the same time, we cannot entirely rule out the seeming miracle of the disciples finding a sudden fluency in languages with which they may have had nodding acquaintance. There are modern examples of this. Yet again, the whole story may have been an attempt to account for the apostles' courage in sallying forth to take the gospel to every corner of the known world. It may be saying, 'Such power came upon them that these simple men were able to make the Lord's message understood as far abroad as Egypt, Rome and Persia!'

Whatever happened, the disciples gained a confidence that now carried them forward, a confidence they had not had before and which they could only attribute to the entry into them of a power from outside. Michael Ramsey took up from me that image of a breaking of the apron-strings:

Jesus revealed God to them and became so utterly the central form that they were clinging to Him. But that could not go on for ever. They had to make a painful transition to a new relationship in which they clung to Him as something within their own lives, and not just as a nostalgic kind of thing. The great story that marks this transition is that of Jesus saying to Mary Magdalen on the Resurrection Day: 'Do not cling to Me, as in the past. It really is Me, but you and my other followers are passing on to a new relationship of a very tremendous kind.'

Which is a touching piece of poetry, but does it make inevitable the invention of this kind of magic ingredient in the Christian faith known as the Holy Spirit? Why is it not just Christ's spirit, God's spirit? Why attach a third wheel to the chariot?

Michael Ramsey brought back the element of *response*. Jesus had made so tremendous an impact on His followers that they wanted to respond with all their powers. And yet those were so puny and futile.

I think the point of the Holy Spirit is this: a divine something in them, enabling their response to the divine above and about them. Now it is so today: if I believe in God and Jesus and want to respond to them – there is a divine something enabling me to do so.

To put it as simply as possible: where is God? God is above us and around us and everywhere, the world's creator. Where is God? God is particularly revealed in Jesus, the very image of God. Where is God? God is within me, enabling me to respond to God above me and around me. Why a person? Because God is always personal, not impersonal, so I find myself saying not that there's an *It* within me – but just as there is a *He* to whom I am responding, so there is a He within me enabling me to make that response.

Then, with a chortle: 'There, in just a minute or so, is Michael Ramsey about the Holy Spirit.'

A response of the God within to the God without, then. But who made this connection? Did He do it, or did we have to make the effort?

As in everything in Christianity, we make the effort and it appears to be our work, but there is the divine in us exciting our effort and making it in us and through us. In absolutely everything in Christianity there is a paradox that it's our doing and yet not our doing.

As usual, I tiptoed respectfully away from the paradox. But I had picked up, once again, a point of unity with my own eccentric Quaker tradition. This notion of the God, the Christ, the light *within* is central to Quakerism, which goes so far as to say that scripture itself is lifeless and dead unless illuminated by that light within the reader, the divine within confirming the divine outside. John Stott, I fancy, would put it the other way round, for when I asked him how we could be sure when the Holy Spirit was breathing into us he came firmly back to the Bible as the starting point:

Because if the Bible is inspired by the Holy Spirit, then He will not speak in a way contradictory to the scriptures. The great Reform theologians all down the centuries have said how important it is to keep the Word of God and the Spirit of God in tandem; because without the Word the Spirit may be an alien spirit. Without the Spirit, the Word is a lifeless and dead letter. The Spirit brings the Word to life; but it's by the Word we check the Spirit's illumination.

So no 'Do-it-yourself' religion. Back to the Bible.

Whatever the gospel writers thought about the distinct reality of the Spirit, St Paul could not conceive of the Church without it; though it seems to me wrong to regard him as in any way sketching out a doctrine of the Trinity. It was the divine influence or breath which gave the Christian community its superhuman power and authority. It could also be something of a nuisance.

There is the passage in Paul's first letter to the Corinthians in which he lists the gifts, or charisms, of the Spirit (hence the Charismatic Movement), which include wisdom, healing, miracle-working prophecy, discerning of spirits, ecstatic utterance and the power to interpret the latter. The Corinthians had obviously been swept by a craze for glossolalia, for while he assures them he is no mean tongue at it himself, yet 'I had rather speak five words with my understanding . . . than ten thousand words in an unknown tongue.' Besides, if everyone utters at once, visitors will think they have all gone mad. Paul greatly prefers prophesying to uttering, pointing out that unless people 'utter by the tongue words easy to be understood . . . ye shall speak into the air.' Besides, there was the problem of getting people to interpret what had been said. This problem still remains, and I have to admit that where I have heard one speaker-in-tongues interpreted by another, I have come away singularly unenlightened. But that may be my fault.

Jack Dominian, the psychiatrist, regards the Protestant tradition in the Charismatic Movement as

A constant attempt to transform God into a tangible reality. Through hearing, through touch, through ecstatic utterances and other very physical experiences, people whose faith cannot be sustained by the unseen and the unknown seek the physically and emotionally recognisable to reinforce their trust.

He is more merciful to the controlled Catholic tradition as 'A means of reaching God through feelings and emotions which were terribly constrained in the Catholic Church before.'

Watson, Cray and Green are more enthusiastic, though also more cautious than they might have been a few years back, when Charismatics got a bad name for insisting that unless you had been baptised by the Holy Ghost, zonked by the Spirit, you were barely a second-class Christian.

Cray says:

The problem of all renewal movements is that if they are not welcomed with open arms, they pull off to one side and slightly overemphasise the things they have to contribute. And yet they need the balancing of the maturity and experience of the rest of the Church.

He emphasises that every way in which a Christian works to build up the Church is a gift of the Spirit. There is no barrier between things like catering and administration on the one hand and healing and speaking in tongues on the other:

Charismatic is from the Greek word for 'grace'. All of Christian life comes about through Christ's forgiveness and is the experience of God's grace. The Charismatic Movement has been trying to take the Church back to its sources of power, to understand its true nature. As for calling 'speaking in tongues' ecstatic: that seems to imply the gift is out of the control of the speaker, and it quite definitely isn't.

That rather surprised me. Michael Green insisted:

Glossolalia sounds very strange to people, and they used to think only lunatics did it. But it's not so. There are thousands and thousands of people – many in our own congregation – who speak in tongues privately, in their own prayers. It's a release, but it isn't an ostensive mark of being a Christian, and nowhere in the New Testament does it suggest it is. It's one of the gifts of the Holy Spirit, but it's not to be dolled up as the main thing.

If you like, it's a love language. I expect when you and I are in bed with our wives at night we have a special sort of love language that we wouldn't like to go out on the BBC. It's intimate, it's personal, and I know that is what speaking in tongues is. It releases people in praise and prayer, and I find it very helpful when you don't know what to pray just to pray in tongues. The Holy Spirit within you is nudging you in that way. But it's not anything to get terribly excited about.

Feeling embarrassed rather than excited, I changed the subject.

David Watson had squirmed at the word 'charismatic', calling it part of the Devil's tactics to tie labels on people. He saw charismatic renewal as fundamentally a greater openness to the Holy Spirit and His works.

Sadly, the institutional Church is not throbbing with vitality. We are faced with either Bible-words or God-words which are pretty empty and meaningless or just tradition and formalism. I believe that part of the renewing work of the Holy Spirit is bringing back something of the joy and love and sense of God's presence which makes people begin to listen to His words. Most people are word-resistant. They need to sense God's reality before they begin to listen to what He may be saying to them.

Couldn't that be rather dangerous, moving into the irrational?

Yes, there is always that danger. When people just want some extra-sensory experience, they can opt for anything, whether it is true or not. For some people any religious experience is equally valid. I keep on quoting the scriptures, so I think words are important. But I think the first impact on the person's inner being often has to be at gut level, even people with a fairly high level of education. There is a gut reaction in the nation today that the Church is irrelevant. That has to be changed to a gut reaction that there is something here after all.

Which, to put it crudely, puts the Holy Spirit in the business of delivering knock-out punches to the solar plexus. This may be an anatomical quibble, but I would prefer to think of It as aiming rather at the heart.

But why should it not be Christ Himself, or His Father, who does so? There are many cases in which, for Spirit, one could as well read 'the Spirit of Christ'; and if Christ was God, it follows that one could equally understand 'the Spirit of God'. A crude explanation for the invention of the Spirit might be the following train of thought: We came to know the true nature of God from His incarnation on earth in Christ. Christ has been taken from us into Heaven. Yet how is it that we are still aware of His presence among us? That must be the Holy Spirit.

However, the Church did not leave it at that. In a sense – I have to keep using that phrase to avoid tedious qualifications – the Holy Spirit was a theological afterthought, a Ghost that came to dinner and stayed on to become a member of the family. A fourth-century heretic named Arius was teaching, in effect, that Jesus was little more than 'God's son', a kind of God Junior or Crown Prince. 'There was', he taught mysteriously, 'when He was not'. The Church stamped on this at the Council of Nicaea, proclaiming that Father and Son were of one substance; and then, since the Spirit was clearly to be seen in the scriptures as the personal activity of God, felt obliged to establish that the Spirit was of that same substance and not inferior either. But, now that the Church was involved in a kind of higher spiritual biology, where did the Spirit come from? The gospel of John implied that it proceeded from the Father through the Son – a concept that should not be strange to any bureaucrat who is accustomed to receiving memoranda from his department head *through* his section leader. But there was a danger here of implying that the Son – the section leader – was subordinate to the Father, a junior again, and the oneness and indivisibility of God had to be maintained – the Jewish tradition of One God against the pagan tradition of many.

Somewhere in Spain in the sixth century a solution was found. There was inserted into the creed the tiny word 'Filioque' – 'and from the Son'. The Spirit, it was now maintained, proceeded from the Father *and from* the Son. In due course the usage spread across France and Germany and was adopted by Rome in the eleventh century. The Christian churches of the East, based on Constantinople, were outraged. They saw it not merely as a subtle theological deviation but as a departure from tradition, a violation of the rule that changes in creed could only be made by a council of the entire Church, and an effort by the Bishop of Rome – the Pope – to establish himself as a dictator over all Christendom. In fact a council held at Florence in 1439 eventually permitted the Spirit to proceed either 'through' *or* 'and from', but with the help of political forces the damage was done and the Great Schism between the churches of East and West remains to this day. Metropolitan Anthony of the Russian Orthodox Church explained to me why, in his view, so small a thing was still so big.

It had been born, he said, of an attempt to improve on a statement by the Lord Jesus Christ Himself.

When the Lord says, 'I will send the Holy Spirit who proceeds from the Father', we might well be content with what God Himself has to say about it. Yet there was an attempt to explain philosophically the way things were. We have always felt there are things we can know from within our own experience, but there are others revealed to us by God because they are simply beyond our direct experience. We should be content with God's revelation. We can try to understand it, but we should not try to improve upon it.

And Metropolitan Anthony went on to reveal the underlying resentment of the Orthodox towards the papal claim of infallibility, a resentment which is unassuaged by Vatican Two's development of 'collegiality' among the Pope and his bishops:

I think it is exactly as objectionable as before, because nothing has changed as far as the Papacy is concerned. Collegiality is completely under the control of the Pope; the College cannot discuss anything which is not placed on the agenda by the Pope, and no decision can be taken which is not ratified by the Pope, so that ultimately, as a consultative body, it has no more authority than it had before.

Political and cultural differences between East and West were probably irreconcilable anyway. But the Great Schism over the origins of the Holy Spirit demonstrates, it seems to me, what is bound to happen when – in the interests of insulating and safeguarding doctrine – men endeavour to contain within human terms what they know to be beyond such terms. I really doubt whether today there is much danger of the faithful turning polytheist if they get the idea that the Holy Spirit is handed down *from* the Father *through* the Son; or whether Christ suffers injury because some of us believe that the Spirit issues simultaneously from Himself and His Father. The fact that such images conjure up bizarre physical tableaux only shows how provisional they are – provisional for those who cannot lightly abandon what their trusted saints have handed down to them, unnecessary for others who can no longer think in those terms.

You will probably have detected by now that in these wanderings through the mysteries of the Spirit, I have not personally found much to take hold of. Two points do make sense to me: that the Spirit is concerned with our communication with God – it is, as it were, the wavelength on which we get in touch with the divine; and that the Spirit is that within us which responds to God. In his book, Lord Ramsey speaks of 'God within responding to God beyond'. This would seem to be a uniquely human gift; it is something given; and if something has been given, there was something to give – namely the Spirit. It seems to me, from my experience, that this is something more than our own active awareness of God – something we make – for there is, as John V. Taylor implies, something *passive* on our part whenever the Spirit strikes within us. I can only try to illuminate these fumblings by quoting two of my victims on the very nature of the religious thing.

It was Peter Baelz who quoted to me the old scholastic tag, 'Nothing is loved unless it is first known.' But, he said,

I'm coming to believe that is less and less true. I came across an American woman philosopher who was converted to Christianity and who found herself loving God before she believed in Him. Again, the metaphysical poet Traherne says there is in all of us, basically, a longing for God which is a response to His love. I think one is drawn by one's intuitions towards the centre; there is something that grasps one like a vision. It is something like falling in love. It is something like listening to a work of music and being wrapped up in it. And then the mind comes into play to check these feelings: theology is a bit like music and musical criticism – the critic listens to the music and criticises it, but he doesn't actually create the music. Without the music, he's no use at all.

Then there was David Jenkins saying he felt more and more that religion was not man-centred but God-centred, the response to a mystery that simply *demanded* our attention and response. But what, I asked him, about the people who argued that it was not a mystery so much as a long chain of problems along which we were gradually working our way?

Certainly there were problems to be solved, Jenkins replied, and the mystery was no excuse for making a muddle of those. But the mystery was to do with the transcendent, the dimension of moving outwards from those problems and situations. I suggested that nowadays it was possible to see Christianity as a richly mythological system which was gradually being replaced by psychological explanations. By no means all the problems were solved yet, but one could sense where it was all heading.

'Well, of course it's a myth,' said Canon Jenkins boldly.

Undoubtedly it's a story made up about the universe in response to this mystery. But a whole pattern of responses built up first on the history of the people who became the Jews, and then upon what some people spotted in Jesus. The gentlemen who think the world will be de-mystified and that we can get all the problems out of the universe seem to me to believe in a much less plausible myth. People who get easily optimistic are missing the hellish possibilities of things, and they haven't spotted the heavenly ones either.

In retrospect, both these theologians were telling me something about the Holy Spirit, about its insistence – often in spite of ourselves – upon straining outwards towards the divine, upon responding to something which is quite strange to us but which is already part of us (there – I have committed a paradox). I think what appealed to me about these two theologians was that they did not do what theologians often do, and that is to appropriate the Spirit exclusively to the Church. One sometimes hears the Spirit spoken of as 'The divine breath in the Body of Christ' (which is the Church), but the decrees of the Second Vatican Council allow that the Holy Spirit was at work in the world even before Christ and in other religions. Whatever it represents (and we shall hear more of that in the following chapter) it is no bird to be locked up in any man's gilded cage.

CHAPTER EIGHT

Three Ways of Being God

> *Holy, holy, holy,*
> *Merciful and mighty,*
> (I sang)
> *God in three persons,*
> *Blessed Trin-it-teee . . .*

More rarely, I buried my nose in my prayer book and stumbled through the impenetrable thickets of the Athanasian Creed:

> And the Catholick Faith is this:
> That we worship one God in Trinity
> And Trinity in Unity;
> Neither confounding the Persons
> Nor dividing the Substance . . .
> The Father uncreate,
> The Son uncreate,
> And the Holy Ghost uncreate.
> The Father incomprehensible,
> The Son incomprehensible,
> And the Holy Ghost incomprehensible,
> The Father eternal,
> The Son eternal,
> And the Holy Ghost eternal.
> And yet they are not three eternals, but one eternal.
> As also there are not three incomprehensibles,
> Nor three uncreated;
> But one uncreated, and one incomprehensible . . .

And so it went on, unsaying everything it had said and then saying it again. Even the Nicene Creed, with its intriguing 'one substance', was easy going compared with that. I was puzzled, also, by what I took to be the warning that you had to be a Roman Catholic if you wanted to be saved.

However, nobody that I can remember throughout my educational days ventured to preach a sermon on the Trinity;

and I arrived at the start of my radio pilgrimage with the nicely polished witticism that the doctrine of the Trinity was like the Victorian piano in the front parlour; nobody played it nowadays, but nobody dared throw it out. I was surprised to meet quite a number of people who insisted that *they* still played it, and that it sounded as sweet as ever to them. One of my Roman Catholic witnesses, Father Butterworth, called it the king of instruments: 'I don't know of any other which is more basic to the whole Christian orchestration.'

And yet I am still not sure that it convinces me, in the sense of being an instinctive part of my feeling about God. Intellectually I can now see the point, or points, to it; and without that understanding I should be less able to appreciate the faith of my fellow Christians. But I doubt if I would find myself in a very different position personally. Nor am I alone in my perplexity.

Raymond Brown, the Baptist, roared with laughter when I spoke of the Trinity as a 'great big prickly paradox' and said it 'blew his mind'. He added: 'If I could button it all up, it wouldn't be important for me at all. That actually makes it easier for me to accept it.'

Once again Stuart Miller was:

absolutely baffled. It's double-Dutch to me. I can make sense of the idea that Jesus was the human face of God, and that when He left there was still a very real presence of God, and if we want to call that the Holy Spirit – fine. But to say that the three are distinct yet unitary – I just find that unnecessary.

Gai Eaton said there was really no hope of the average Moslem being able to make sense of the Christians' claim that they worshipped not three gods but one. And Rabbi Hugo Gryn said no religious Jew could possibly justify the Trinity or see how it could function. No matter how often the creeds said God was one as often as they said God was three, one, surely was one. 'The Hebrew word we use is a very strong *one*: it is unity, uniqueness, indivisibility. It brings together matter and spirit, form and content, creator and creation.'

But Rabbi Lionel Blue thought he could begin to understand what Christians meant – thanks to a chance encounter in a cafe in Germany.

I saw a boy and a girl speaking loving words to each other across a table; and there was a Marlene Dietrich record going on the juke box – 'Where have all the flowers gone?'. The boy and girl were looking soulfully into each other's eyes, and I suddenly realised that they formed a strange kind of unity; that for a moment the boy and the girl and the song were one. And then I could understand the Trinity: that the love between two people can unify them, and I began to get *some* idea of what the Christian means: there was the Father and the Son and the Holy Ghost – the love between them that connects them.

I am quite sure Rabbi Blue was not about to introduce Trinitarianism into his synagogue, but he had caught on to an explanation I was to hear confirmed by Christian witnesses.

To put it uncharitably, the doctrine of the Trinity is a way of helping Christianity out of a hole – by asserting that it is not a hole at all but in fact the Way. Like its Jewish progenitor, Christianity declares there is but one God. But He has a Son – *and* He has sent His Holy Spirit among men. Yet there is only one God. The three are distinct, yet they are one. The First Vatican Council's Dogmatic Constitution on the Catholic Faith (of 1870) declares that this is an 'absolute mystery' – something that has been revealed by God as true, but which is beyond human powers to understand. You might say it 'blows the mind', and while it is easy enough to mock at this, I do not think it unreasonable to say there are things beyond our reasoning whose existence we do not doubt.

But where does the doctrine originate? Some trace it back to the threefold cry in Isaiah of 'Holy, holy, holy . . .' or to 'the God of Abraham, of Isaac, and of Jacob'; others to the juxtaposition in the baptism by John of Jesus, the dove of the Holy Spirit and the voice of God the Father; while others again rest upon the instruction, attributed to Jesus in the closing verses of Matthew, to baptise 'in the name of the Father, and of the Son, and of the Holy Ghost' (though I should have thought that was open to the charge of being a later addition).

John Stott, who is as biblical a Christian as any I have met, does not find the Trinity as a developed doctrine anywhere in the Bible. The very word is not to be found in it. But neither is the term 'sacrament'. 'There are many words that we use as a convenient shorthand,' says Stott.

Nevertheless, I *do* find the Trinity in the New Testament, historically revealed. The first followers of Jesus were, of course, all Jews, brought up to believe the Lord their God was one God, and you must love the Lord your God with all your being. Then, as they spent time in the company of Jesus, they came to be convinced that He was more than man and called Him Lord, which was a divine title. But then Jesus complicated it further by speaking to them of somebody else coming, called the Holy Spirit, who took His place on the day of Pentecost. So the unavoidable facts of their own historical experience led them to believe in the Father, the Son and the Holy Spirit.

That sounds simple enough; except that it would seem to point towards a kind of miniature Greek Olympus, with three distinct figures seated on the heavenly mountain-top. And that, as every Jew knew, was blasphemous. Every Christian, I think, knows that it is not like that, either. And yet, *as* we know it, some of us find ourselves slipping into curious mental pictures. The best I could manage, for years, was an image of the godhead as a single three-sided prism, or as a statue with three faces, like the sublime Hindu *trimurti* in the cave temples of Elephanta. This, however, is open to objection for being too monolithic, too static, too lacking in the very contradictions that make the Trinity what is is. Even so progressive a theologian as Dennis Nineham (one of the 'Myth of God Incarnate' group) insists that he is no Unitarian, in the historical sense of the term, and that he and his colleagues

would want to find values in Trinitarian theology, even though they might not say Jesus is supernatural in the traditional Trinitarian sense. They might say a pure statement that Jesus was just a man won't do justice to the riches we find in the tradition.

Jack Dominian finds a psychological truth among those riches. Each one of us, he says, begins life as a helpless baby fused to our mother and father. Some twenty years of growth separates us from them and gives us a separate identity. Thereafter, all our relationships depend upon a tension between fusion and separation. To be a mature human it is necessary to retain our identity as a separate person and yet to fuse with others at recurrent intervals.

Dominian goes on: 'At the very heart of the Trinity is this profound psychological reality of three totally separate persons who are constantly fused with one another without ever losing their separateness.'

Then is the Trinity, in effect, Father, Mother and Child?

But Jack Dominian is a Catholic as well as a psychiatrist.

You can call them Father, Mother, Child if you like – that's a very lovely symbolic expression. But it's not an acceptable one because you define one as child when in fact they are all equal. You can have Father, the source of creation; Son, the source of salvation; Spirit, the source of grace and revelation to all of us. What in fact the ultimate characteristics are is a mystery. What is not a mystery – and is paramount for humanity – is the symbol of relationship, because in essence it is three separate persons who are constantly relating in love, totally available to one another, but never get lost in each other. And at the heart of human love, too, is total availability but never the loss of self in another.

This I find satisfying for a while; and then the satisfaction begins to wear off. For surely the love relationship in human beings is essentially *two*-sided, not three; and if you call the relationship itself a third person, you are both doing violence to the concept of person and making that third a junior product of the first two.

What we have run into here, I suspect, was best described by Professor McQuarrie: 'I think where people have problems with the Trinity is when they begin to take some of the words too literally, as for instance these Three Persons: they begin to think of it as a kind of committee.' For McQuarrie, the Trinity makes a lot of sense. He sees it as the peculiarly Christian way of thinking about God.

God has been conceived in many different ways. But when the Christian says God is Father, Son and Holy Spirit, there's a great deal packed into that. The whole notion about God being immanent in the world as well as transcendent: that's all taken care of in this doctrine.

Father Butterworth, having expressed his surprise that I bothered with the doctrine of the Trinity – 'It's so out of fashion' – warmed to it with enthusiasm:

It's the root truth about the Christian God. Without it, intelligent and sympathetic understanding of the faith lacks much of a basis: because the Trinity represents what is *new* in the Christian revelation. Otherwise it is very difficult to see what all this fuss is about.

Go on, I said: why was it necessary first to divide God up and then stick Him together again?

Father Butterworth sighed and observed – with the *greatest* of respect – that that was the very travesty of the doctrine which had gained so much currency.

I think it's terribly important to realise that you are not dealing with some kind of celestial conundrum about how three persons can still be one. It is the basic Christian mystery: a self-revealed truth about how God actually is in Himself. When we call it a mystery we mean this truth will never be adequately understood or expressed in human formulations. What we are saying is that God reveals Himself in Jesus as a God of relationship. A God who is the Father of Jesus, who is His personal Son. That this relationship between Father and Son is the Holy Spirit – the power and presence of God. And that this trinity is an expression of the reality of God, into which each Christian is invited to come and share in the relationship. Now that's a very crude way of expressing the doctrine of the Trinity.

I tried to be cruder still. What was wrong with saying that God was the Father all right; Jesus a very special prophet; and the Holy Spirit the influence of God still with us?

Father Butterworth acknowledged that was what a good many Christians thought.

But it does not seem to me to express the real novelty about the

Christian God, which is His intense intimacy with man. I think what you say misses that. Holding, as I do, to the personal divinity of Jesus, any other expression of who He was and what He stood for is inadequate to the basic Christian experience.

Father Butterworth applauded my observation that it is still an offence under the Blasphemy Act of 1697 to doubt the Trinity. But why, I persisted, did the average churchgoer fail to be grabbed by the doctrine?

Father Butterworth thought it a fact that, in many respects, Latin Christian theology had got further and further away from the original experience.

The primary emphasis has been on the *unity* of God. I suppose it springs from a time when Christians were still converting polytheists, and felt that this great stress on oneness was characteristic of themselves. But it began to affect the general course of theology to the extent that even in quite recent textbooks the assumption is that God is first one and then, by the way, you have to remember that He is also three. This seems to me a totally topsy-turvy presentation of the revelation we are meant to pick up from Jesus.

Could it be that Father Butterworth actually fancied a mild flirtation with polytheism? Perish the thought! But where, in scripture, could he find justification for the Trinity?

Clearly you're not going to be able to justify it by finding it in so many explicit terms: that would be an anachronism. However, I think you find it is Jesus' own experience of God, characterised by this intimacy with the Father. The elements are there, I think, even in the gospel picture of Jesus; to say nothing of the more explicit ways in which St Paul talks – much earlier than the written gospels that we have. If you look at the eighth chapter of Romans and see what is said, I think you will find that the elements of the later doctrine can be discovered there.

I re-read Romans, chapter 8, and it was true. The elements of God, Christ and the Spirit were subtly interwoven. But there was still no clarification that they were of equal status and not, as it were, President, Vice-President and Secretary of State. But again, I suppose, I was committing the error of approaching the Trinity as a kind of committee, rather than (as one of the early theologians put it) 'three ways of being God', a more active figure of speech than 'three dimensions'.

It must be significant that although the doctrine of the Trinity was nailed down in the Nicene Creed by the end of the fourth century, the Feast of the Trinity was only made general for the Western Church in 1334. To this day, the Church of England has some nice hymns for it but has failed to lift it above being one of the dimmer festivals in the calendar: a dreary milestone with no attractions of its own.

But for the speculative approach of Greek philosophy, trying to push metaphysical reasoning to its limits, the Church might have done without the elaborate formulations that we have today. Hans Küng points out that Father, Son and Spirit are described as present at the martyrdom of Stephen – God as glory, Jesus standing at God's right hand, and the Holy Spirit filling Stephen: but Küng shows a certain impatience with later 'philosophisings' which he finds remote from the New Testament – the arguments about essence, substance, subsistence and relations which filled the early councils of the Church.

I cannot help sharing Professor Küng's impatience, but it is too late to go back now to the days of the apostles. Not only has too much piety and faith been invested in the doctrine; too much spiritual insight has been stimulated and expressed through it for us to afford throwing it away. What may be questioned today, however, is whether we are assisted in exploring our own experience by trying to say what we mean in terms devised for a quite different intellectual age.

But are there any better terms? As I noted in an earlier chapter, Professor John Bowker finds a link between the Trinity and modern 'information theory'. He says:

Everything else flows from it. It's the one truly profound insight that Christianity has contributed; and we can see that, because of what we now understand this universe to be – a constant transaction of available energy being used to build up complicated organisations of atoms, from planets to such strange and beautiful things as

Margaret Thatcher, Racquel Welch and you and me. Every stage of this process has led to new levels of relationship and interaction with which we can relate and interact.

Now what I believe is that the human organisation of energy is able to enter into an even wider range of relationships, including the environment of God. And if this universe is derived from God, and if there are any clues in this universe, then God must be relational in Himself. You couldn't have a universe like this, in which relatedness is the fundamental property, unless relationship were derived from His own being.

But why does it have to be a trinity?

In terms of information theory, the basic conditions are trinitarian. Using the technical jargon, you have to have two poles of reciprocity and a channel of communication between them. Those are the minimum conditions of relationship, the means of life at all. Father and Son, with the Holy Spirit as the channel of communication between them. In less jargonistic language, if the Trinity did not exist, it would be necessary to invent it.

So perhaps those wordy Greek theologians, whose debates are said to have spread to the very barbers' shops of Constantinople, did better than I was prepared to grant.

Even my Quaker friend Kenneth Barnes was prepared to defend the Trinity:

I was trained as a scientist and I can't stop being one; but the Trinity runs through my life, not in an impersonal way but a personal one. I see it as an excellent way of formulating a belief, both for its time and to some extent for the present.

Peter Baelz of Durham sees the doctrine as answering the objection that God is too far above us to be comprehensible at all.

What attracts me about the gospels is the sense that this mysterious, incomprehensible God is, at the same time, nearer to us than breathing. Though I wouldn't go to the stake for the doctrine of the Trinity – and I don't believe in the doctrine of the Trinity – I believe in what the doctrine is trying to express. I think it is trying to say that God is *both*: He who is beyond our understanding, but He who gives

128

Himself to us through His creation, redemption and spirit; so that God is both beyond and within. I won't let go of either of these poles.

Valerie Fisher is well aware she is using words that any linguistic philosopher could tear apart,

But I have a working picture of the Trinity, and it's a movement – a movement from the totally incomprehensible into my very concrete, limited, time-bounded life – a movement so that God becomes something I can relate to and comprehend. But it doesn't stop there. He didn't say, 'All right, I've given you a good example – now push off and do what you can!' We were told: 'You can have my Spirit; you are my body on earth; you are in Christ.' I feel it is Christ's Spirit, continuing the Spirit of God, becoming part of us all to take us back to God, in a way which I couldn't describe without using the same old doctrinal terms. But I see it as a movement from God to me, lifting me back up with it. So that, in a way, the Trinity becomes a four-sided thing rather than just three – with me in the Trinity.

We seem to have gone now from unity through binity and trinity to quaternity: but perhaps it is as misleading to think of God in numerical terms as it was to think of Him as a committee. Some Eastern theologians have argued that rather than three stars in a triangle, the Trinity should be thought of as three in line, one in front of the other, each giving light to the one before it and producing for humanity a single, indistinguishable glory.

Archbishop Blanch made his run-up through the Old Testament, where

The Spirit was the actual breath of God Himself, animating and giving life to the human body, and spiritual life as well. The Old Testament writers did not personalise the Spirit, though; they thought of it primarily as a force which invades and inspires a person but has no independent existence.

I'm sure that in the early stages of the New Testament their understanding was akin to the Old. So when Our Lord talks about casting out demons by the Spirit of God, they would have meant nothing more than they did by Elijah healing the sick by the Spirit of God, or being carried up into Heaven by it. But they were in the grip of a theological inevitability. Once having come to terms with the fact that they worshipped Christ on a par with their God, then inevitably the road was open for extending that further; and with their own powerful experience of the Holy Spirit not just as a force but as an indwelling experience, then I think they saw no reason why they should not personalise the Spirit too.

They all began with a fanatical devotion to the One God, as opposed to the polytheism of their Greek, Syrian and Canaanite neighbours. They move on to the conviction that they cannot with-hold divine honours from Christ, and they worship Him in their liturgies. Then they move on into the experience of Pentecost – not just a historical experience, but a personal one – so at that point you are in the presence of a fully developed *experience* of trinity, which ultimately takes trinitarian theological forms.

Stuart Blanch allowed himself to speculate that if Christian theology had remained within the Hebrew framework, the doctrine of the Trinity might never have been expressed as it is now.

But it would still have been an enormous problem . . . It clearly was one of the causes of the breach between Judaism and Christianity. I suppose the theology would have grown up in a more personal, less conceptual way. It might have had a firmer base in experience, and rather less in ratiocination. Once you base it in actual spiritual experience, it does make some sense. You have to say it is an inadequate expression of that experience, but it does correspond to something.

Here the Archbishop added a remark that ought to be printed on every page of this book:

As most of us have to be able to articulate our faith in some way, however inadequate, this is as good a way as any. I think this is a question of the limitations of theology: it is a very poor instrument for recording a very profound experience.

The experience may not even be terribly profound. Father Timothy Firth recalled his struggle with a sixth-form girl who protested that she 'Didn't believe in all this doctrine stuff about trinities and things.' 'So,' said Father Firth, 'I told her to think for a minute or two about what God is. And she wrote down, "God somehow started it all. It's got something to do with Jesus. And He's still around." And I reckon that's a pretty good definition of the Trinity.'

Maybe. But I doubt whether that girl would admit to believing that the Holy Ghost is of the Father and of the Son, neither made nor created nor begotten, but proceeding; or that in all things the Unity in Trinity and Trinity in Unity is to be worshipped – such being required for salvation. As we have seen, there *are* convinced trinitarians among us; but I still have the impression that most believers are either instinctive unitarians or binitarians or even bitheists, regarding the Holy Spirit as another term for the presence of God.

The late Professor Geoffrey Lampe – one of the kindest of theologians when confronted with an amateur like myself – said frankly that he could not see much future for the doctrine of the Trinity. It was not that it was false, but that as a model to help us grasp a reality beyond our comprehension, it no longer served its purpose for many of the faithful. Professor Lampe wanted to rethink the model, though not the faith it was intended to express: he did not want a unitarianism that denied the divinity of Christ, and he granted that at least Trinitarianism had the advantage of making it impossible to oversimplify God's mystery. Lampe saw God in terms of a continuous operation, creating, redeeming and sanctifying: but then, he may not have heard of information theory.

Again, I have sympathy with this; though it leads us close to the 'Myth of God Incarnate' view, that Jesus did not claim to be the literal only son of God, and that the doctrine of Him as God in human flesh is a myth in the sense of being a poetic effort to express the meaning of Him elaborated by those who did not know Him personally. Don Cupitt, another of the group, insisted that the doctrine of Incarnation distorted the message of Jesus by creating a cult of the divine Christ which has pushed God the Father into the background, where Jesus never intended Him to be.

Rumbling away beneath all this, it seems to me, is the division between those who regard religion as *objective* –

something factual revealed to us from outside – and those who see it as *subjective* – discovered within ourselves. Don Cupitt himself has suggested it is time we took leave of the authoritative, objective God and exercised our own private spiritual autonomy. At no time is it more tempting to agree with Cupitt than when punch-drunk after sparring with the Trinity.

Now I hear the call of religious liberty as clearly as anyone, and am sceptical about the wisdom of insisting that people ought to believe things which (it seems to me) we do not all *know*. Some of us may believe them, we may trust in them, but when we say, 'You *ought* to believe this' we are really saying, 'If you were like me, you *would* believe this.' We are plainly not all alike, however.

On the other hand, we are not all so dissimilar, either. Enough of us have shared the same experiences of the divine, and the same way of thinking about it, to have evolved what we call the Christian Faith. As it now stands, that faith is understood and expressed in trinitarian terms, terms that have served at least sixteen centuries of mostly worthy people very well; and we have heard other good people advance contemporary arguments for believing they may continue to do so. To scrap that terminology would not be throwing out the baby with the bathwater so much as throwing out the bath and leaving the baby high and dry.

Nor is it so simple as subjective versus objective. Of course there is an element of subjectivity in our religious life – there is personal subjectivity and what I have called the collective subjectivity. But if objectivity does not exist in the same sense in which there is an objective cat in the garden, Christians do believe (many would say *know*) that there is something out there and in here which they call God, and which is being God in three distinct ways.

I think I am right in saying that Christianity is the only one of the world's great religions to have developed such categorical creeds. It felt obliged to make itself distinct from both paganism and Judaism, and this involved working out a difficult blend of historical fact, metaphysical philosophy and religious symbolism. The insistence – which I believe to be a profound insight – that good works were not enough to secure integrity, that justification was by faith, made it necessary to define 'faith in *what*'. As the 1976 Doctrine Commission of the Church of England argued, the creeds were very far from being dry as dust when they were first hammered out; they were seen as safeguarding the true interpretation of scripture, rather than creating original doctrine. But the problems they sought to answer were contemporary problems – contemporary to the fourth to sixth centuries – and the errors they strove to exclude were not necessarily those that would bother us now. If the creeds were to be written today, they would probably have much more to say about the personality of Jesus and the meaning of the Eucharist (which is not mentioned at all in the creeds we now have).

The trinitarian creeds did their best to exclude error, but we should never forget that it was acknowledged at the time that they were an attempt to express what was inexpressible; in the honest and eloquent words of St Augustine, 'They are only an alternative to silence.'

CHAPTER NINE

The Church You Love to Hate

With rare exceptions among Trappists and Quakers, silence is not very popular in church; or outside it. While church-goers spend much of their time describing God, praising God and petitioning Him, non-churchgoers have plenty to say about why the churchgoers are phonies: they burn people at the stake for heresy, *fail* to burn people at the stake for heresy, represent the Tory party at prayer, represent the Communist party in the pulpit, lavish vast sums on vestments and palaces, tell fairy stories that none of them believes, call each other names, frighten little children with threats of hell-fire, cause civil war in Ireland and pretend to be better than others when in fact they are just as bad. Anyway, we are told, nobody goes to church any more.

In fact that is not true. As many people patronise the churches of Britain as the football grounds; membership seems to have taken an upward turn of late and applications for the ministry are on the increase in most churches. The truth of the notion that we have lapsed from a profoundly religious country to a cynically irreligious one in the course of the past century is very dubious. I doubt if we were ever as devout as the Latin nations, and you have only to read Chaucer to see how deep is our native scepticism of the Church and the clergy.

And yet we – England and Scotland – both have national churches which show no signs of becoming disestablished. The General Synod of the Church of England is a comparatively recent institution, handicapped by class habits and proximity to the Houses of Parliament; but the General Assembly of the Church of Scotland has long fancied itself as the authentic national forum.

Dr Andrew Ross told me:

The Kirk still plays a significant role in the life of Scotland, can still get a great furore over some ecclesiastical issue, even an Scots who don't go to church very often. This is partly an historic hangover. But in many working-class housing estates, although church attendance is not high, the minister is often better known and accepted and less a figure of fun than the English vicar. Of course, I know many Church of England vicars do a superb job, but I'm talking of the image. The Kirk doesn't dictate and dominate morally as once it did, although unfortunately there are still some ministers who would like to; but I think it still plays a real if diminishing part in the life of Scotland.

Frank Gibson, the Church of Scotland's Director of Social Work, with a budget of seven million pounds behind him, thought the Kirk's claim to power all came down to professionalism. As one of the largest providers of residential social care in Scotland, it could tell the government what it knew from experience, 'which no one can better. Now that is power,' he added. But

my colleagues outside the Church accuse us invariably of two things: one is being trivial, and the other is being mediocre. And God save us from both, because many of the things the General Assembly discusses are quite trivial. Mediocrity I can't stand. The whole thing is passing us by.

Did Mr Gibson think the Church of England a bit wet in comparison?

I find the further south I go from Inverness – never mind Edinburgh – there's a God worshipped that is called Consensus. Once, at a government committee meeting in London, I moved a motion; and a radical councillor from Camden said he hoped I wouldn't do it again because that particular committee had never voted motions. Now I found that an alien way of thinking. This desire to get consensus is a Church of England attitude which may be appropriate for them, but for me – I don't think the answer is in consensus.

Dr Ross pointed out that for a long time it had been established that the General Assembly alone decided doctrine,

...day the Church of England could not alter ... without Parliament getting in on the act, as ... to do very recently in defence of the glories of ...urgy.

...th of England, with its twenty-six guaranteed seats ... ...shops in the House of Lords (a privilege denied to any other church) is not exactly indifferent to power, but likes to think of its influence as being more spiritual. It is also, *de facto*, the custodian of a considerable part of the national heritage. Not many bishops live in real palaces – though a few do, such as those of York, Canterbury, Wells, Durham and Peterborough, and surely nobody would want to see those fall down – mostly they live in houses big enough to receive and entertain in, and old enough to be a considerable burden on their wives. As for the cathedrals, Dean Sydney Evans of Salisbury points out that, unlike the French, the British state takes no responsibility for them at all; it is left entirely to the Dean and Chapter to raise the money to keep the place up.

What attitude should one take to an inheritance of that kind which is, after all, the creation of Christian faith? People seem to want to come in large numbers, and you've got to do the best you can to enable them to go away again with something of a vision that they hadn't got before.

Dean Evans admits that the image of the homeless friar, wandering the road in brown habit and sandals, has its attractions; but he still thinks that modern man values something with more cultural depth, with architecture, music and art.

Guildford cathedral is one of the latest, and maybe last, of the great Anglican cathedrals. Its Dean, Tony Bridge, firmly believes that modern man

is far more hungry for some sort of transcendent vision, some sort of splendour, than he is for practicalities – of which he has an abundance. I would have thought every penny spent on cathedrals is worth it. I think the vast crowds who come to them find they are linked by them with their past, with the history of their country, and with a vision – however inarticulate – of something which they don't have and would love to have. I think it is immensely moving.

Bishop Reindorp admits the Church of England is lucky to have the income from its investments of a thousand million pounds, but demands

How many on the pay-roll? I would say about fifteen thousand plus several thousand pensioners. You cite the Church Commissioners owning all this property, but nobody ever talks about the pay-roll and the vicarages to be kept up. And who does it come from? People of the past who loved God and wanted their money to be used for His service.

You can take another knock at the Established Church for its bureaucracy and its endless synodising. But Christian Howard, who has worked for the Church of England since the 1940s, retorts quite sharply that the General Synod is an improvement on what it used to be and, if some of its members do play politics, 'I don't think the game is as pantomime-like as over the way' – by which she means the House of Commons.

For the Church of England does have parties of its own, notably the Anglican Catholic wing, or High Church, and the Evangelical wing. In between there is a broad middle ground, the traditional heart of the Anglican Church, to which George Reindorp belongs. Like all middle-of-the-roaders, he finds himself at odds with the extremes:

I wholeheartedly welcome the shot in the arm that the charismatics have given the Church. But I must say I resent intensely the feeling too many of them give that if you haven't had their experience, you're a second-class Christian. I mean, St. Paul was 'seized of the Spirit' but, my goodness, he had some intellectual capacity to test his experience; and that sometimes is lacking. If somebody tells me that when I was baptised it didn't mean anything until I was born again, I think that's bordering on arrogance about what the Holy Spirit can or cannot do.

As for conservative evangelicals, who seem to make up a considerable majority of those coming forward for ordination nowadays, whereas many of them have first-class brains and are prepared to listen to the opinions of others, I find too large a number are not in that category. When you have young men who have been in the ministry about two minutes declaring, 'You, bishop, are wrong!', you hold tight on to your chair and think 'Chum – you've got to learn'. What worries me about some of the conservative evangelicals is that they don't seem to know enough about sin. That means they can be so easily thrown in pastoral situations, because they haven't enough experience of the world. How can I say this with gentleness? I would wish there had been an occasion when they had been assailed by some doubt and had to fight it through.

The evangelicals, however, go roaring on. I found that the main threats, as they saw them, came not from the High Church but from modernist theologians like the 'Myth of God Incarnate' school, and from oriental sects like Sun Myung Moon's Unification Church and the Maharishi Mahesh Yogi's Transcendental Meditation movement. Michael Green has written a book called *I Believe in Satan's Downfall* in which he describes them, together with Fascism, Marxism and Maoism, as 'counterfeit religions which provide Satan with a garment of light'. Jack Dominian sees them in more psychological terms:

This happens constantly when you have a transitional period – a vacuum. The various processes which started in the Reformation and are not yet complete are meeting an immature psychological response. It encourages leaders who will act as mummies and daddies telling their followers what to do. The hunger to be told what to do is massive: we have the Iron Lady as our prime minister, and people flock to an authoritarian figure because they are afraid of their own freedom.

Dr Dominian took much the same approach to the growth of Christian fundamentalism, which he found among Catholics as well as Protestants.

I see the invitation that all the churches have made to their people, to grow, to develop a mature conscience and become responsible for their faith, as an extraordinarily threatening invitation to which quite a lot of people are totally unable to respond. The only way they can cling to their faith is to seek absolute authority through the Bible or the Pope. There is a powerful instinct in society, whether we are Christians or not, to find constant daddies telling us what to do. The much smaller element saying, 'Let us become autonomous people, responding to the Church and to God with our own conscience and insight', is still a minority not large enough to be influential in Christianity.

It is the complaint of some that the Church of England no longer knows or dares to tell what anyone ought to do. But Archbishop Runcie still reckons that a national church can 'assist a people to aspire to what it claims to be. It is good to have a group of leaders and priests who have a sense of responsibility not only for the faithful but the not-so-faithful and the don't-knows.'

When I teased the Archbishop about that formidable catalogue of doctrine known as the Thirty-nine Articles – unchangeable without the approval of Parliament – he said they did exclude some evils and superstitions that *he* would want excluded,

But I wouldn't regard them as valid tests of faith today.

I believe that Anglicanism, like Orthodoxy, is a case of living in a certain tradition, in a certain way of worship and pastoral care, and that it is not dependent upon particular confessions of faith which everybody has to subscribe to, or particular authority focused in Rome or Constantinople.

Was the Church of England still Protestant, then? 'Oh yes, it has got a protestant element, in the sense that it has protested and continues to protest against some of the claims of the Papacy.' One of the claims of the Papacy, promulgated by Leo XIII in his document *Apostolicae Curae* (1896) is that the Anglican priesthood is null and void: a matter of acute embarrassment to the leadership of both churches in England, and of some nonsense when it has become virtually routine for successive Popes and Archbishops to embrace each other as brothers. However, Rome is not budged in a day.

It regards its split with the Eastern Orthodox churches – whose priesthood it does recognise – as organisational and historic rather than doctrinal (though Metropolitan Anthony had doubts about that). Rome's differences with the reformed churches of the West involve some very obvious partings over doctrine as well as about who has authority over whom. However, the Second Vatican Council did moderate Rome's claim to be the one true Church, allowing that Catholics, Orthodox, Anglicans and Protestants alike were all members of the Body of Christ. The Council did not grant that all churches were equal, but it did at last refer to them as *churches*, and since then Rome has treated the Anglican church as a favoured, if junior, sister.

But what *is* the Church? We read of it as the People of God, the Body of Christ, the Bride of Christ, Our Holy Mother, the Temple of the Holy Spirit, the Fellowship of All Believers, the Army of God . . . To some it is a sinister hierarchy seeking to enforce its discipline, to others a fellowship of free souls, to some open, to others closed, to some invisible, to others defiantly visible.

Time and again, my victims gave two definitions. It is *my* church or *your* church, for we cannot deny that there are many institutions; but at the same time it is all those who acknowledge the Lordship of Christ. The four church leaders at my round table spoke of it as follows:

Archbishop Runcie:

Of course there will be people who say, 'I prefer Jesus, but I'm not so sure about the Church.' Those who try to live out the impossibilities of Jesus' example are bound, from time to time, to appear hypocritical travesties of the original message, I agree. But I think that in order to give shape and direction to the mission of the Church – the injection of the Christ spirit into the world around us – you've got to operate with an institution.

Lesslie Newbigin (United Reformed):

I think the great difficulty about the *invisible* church is that one always chooses the members oneself. The invisible church is a kind of extension of the ego. The very essence of the Church is that it is a visible body, and it is *one* body. So what do you do about this fragmentation? According to our own theologies the other churches ought to have disappeared, withered on the branch, because they are not true. But why don't they? Not because of any inherent goodness of their own, but because of the mercy of God. Therefore one has to accept this extraordinary illogicality of God's mercy to sinners and, on that basis, seek to listen to one another.

Lord Soper:

Speaking from the standpoint of Methodism, in which I was reared, we were more interested in a particular church than in the general concept. The process in the beginning is the concentration on a particular group of people animated by a certain basic faith. Sooner or later you've got to analyse what you mean by 'the Church', but I think it's probably a secondary process. But I don't think I was ever a member of a divided church. For me, Methodism is a preaching order within the Holy Catholic Church – I wish it would get back to that. When separation means pride of place or holier-than-thou, of course it is an abomination: it prevents the fellowship of all believers. Those who confess the risen Christ must belong to a fellowship which goes far beyond the individual circumstances which separate them.

Cardinal Hume:

In the early Christian community, the Church were witnesses to the resurrection of the Lord. Once you say 'I witness to the resurrection of Jesus Christ' you have said an enormous amount. It's from that act of faith that everything else follows.

Here there seemed so little dissension, so much agreement, that I wondered if the One Great Church did not already exist? Said the Cardinal:

I believe the great church already exists and is broken up scandalously into pieces. There is a profound unity among all of us in so far as we believe in Christ and are baptised. If we are baptised, we already have a unity in the mystical body of Christ. On another level, as that unity needs a visible expression – which is the institution – it's there that the fragmentation takes place. It's the recognition of our oneness through baptism which is going to be the foundation of our institutional unity.

Must there, then, be one unified and visible expression of the faith?

'Well, I think there must,' said the Cardinal.

Because we are supposed to preach the gospel to those who have not yet heard it, or have heard and rejected it; and in so far as our voice is not one, to that extent the force of the message is diminished.

Lord Soper thought there were two possible roads to unity – one monarchical, which had never much appealed to him, and the other federal, which he preferred, given the underlying unity of baptism. Father Basil pushed further:

I do think the unity which is required of us in the institutional church is a unity of faith. We have to agree on those things that have been revealed to us and understand them in the same way, and we have to have unity in our sacramental practice. Because I believe that the faith and the sacraments are central to the life of the Church and always have a visible expression.

Bishop Newbigin put in a word here for the Orthodox churches' approach of mutual commitment to each other in council, while leaving each other free to develop their own styles locally. But the unity of the earlier statements was drifting apart. It would be possible to agree, said Dr Runcie, with all that had been said about baptism – 'almost a magical entry into a cooperative group of congenial people' – whereas 'The sticking point is what sort of tests of faith should exist for those to be judged truly baptised into Christ, and not just to have passed through a ceremony?' Even Lord Soper agreed there must be tests of faith, though he made an impassioned distinction between what he called 'the basic factor of eucharistic worship and the various theories that have been attached to it.' (Of which, more in Chapter 11.)

The Church, then, remains churches; though they are far better neighbours than they have ever been in the past. Said Michael Ramsey:

I do indeed say that a great church already exists. We are now more aware that we are all Christians, and there is much less of 'I'm an

Anglican – you're a Presbyterian'. The decline of the old fussy self-consciousness has been a great feature of these times. Despite our wicked divisions, there is a unity which is a fact.

You have only to read the letters of Paul or the wranglings of the earliest theologians to realise that there has *never* been complete doctrinal harmony among Christians. Nor has there in any other great religion, not even Islam or Judaism. I have dared to suggest, in my image of the mountain, that it would be a bad thing if there were, for it would narrow the panorama of God. Although it might look cost-effective on paper to have only one Church spreading the gospel through the world, it is open to doubt whether such a Church would actually appeal to more people. Nor is bigger necessarily more efficient.

It is possible to justify visible unity by appeal to the twenty-second chapter of John, 'That they all may be one . . .' But as Raymond Brown, the Baptist, observed:

It just depends what you mean by 'one'. I am one with my wife, but we have individual interests that don't harm our relationship – they make it better. I'm not too enamoured of church unity discussions if in the end they mean uniformity – which, I fear, sometimes they do.

Howard Williams, minister of Bloomsbury Central Baptist Church, added:

I'm a bit bothered, sometimes, about the way in which theologians agree too rapidly with one another nowadays. I think there needs to be the cutting edge of recognising that there are areas of very real disagreement as well as of agreement.

Williams could have been referring to the consultations which have been going on for some years now between the Anglicans and the Roman Catholics. Caryl Micklem, the United Reformed minister in central Oxford, was directly critical of the Covenant for Unity worked out between his own church, the Church of England and others, based on the mutual acceptance of bishops:

I feel it's a very one-sided affair. The terms on which our ministry and membership are being accepted seem to me indistinguishable from an Anglican takeover. If I had wanted to be an Anglican, I could have been one years ago. If the Covenant happens, so far as the United Reformed, the Methodists and the Moravians are concerned, the distinctive emphases of Reformed churchmanship will gradually disappear. Someone put it very graphically the other day by saying that if we entered this Covenant we should be appointing captains to lead us back into Egypt, only to discover, perhaps, that the Egyptians wouldn't have us back.

Round the corner from Micklem's church, Michael Green the evangelical Anglican found the ecumenical manoeuvres of the British churches very petty compared with the excitement of Third World Christianity, where:

Deep calls to deep, there's the spirit within you and the spirit within them and it just binds you together in one . . . I've been on the Churches Unity Commission and all those covenanting things; and it is so dull, so dreary, all these people fighting from their corners – nobody lost in wonder, love and praise. I don't find people concentrating on the scriptures and the spirit. It's clinical – rooms filled with cigar smoke, you know. It's a different world from where it's actually happening. In Peru, new house churches full of new believers from absolutely destitute backgrounds. Nobody says, 'Are you a Roman Catholic or are you a Protestant?' The question is odious!

There are house churches in Britain, too, but the question still gets asked. I have to say, for myself – and with all respect to those for whom it remains vitally important – that it seems one of the less helpful factors to introduce, because so many people still think in outdated stereotypes or half-truths. As John McQuarrie put it:

Protestants need to re-educate themselves in what Roman Catholics have believed, and Roman Catholics to re-educate themselves in what Protestants have believed. So often we have assigned views which the other side is supposed to hold, but if one probes beyond that you find it is not really what was intended.

A remarkable number of Protestants still think the Roman

Catholic Church commands its people to believe its doctrines or suffer hell-fire. But 'That image belongs to another age,' says Father Timothy Wright of Ampleforth. 'The Church cannot condemn individuals. There's no way anyone, be he Pope, bishop or priest, can point a finger at another individual, inside or outside the Church, and say, "You are doomed to hell fire!" '

I made another of my efforts to get branded a heretic. But Father Wright declined: 'I think any person who acts faithfully according to his conscience is moving towards his reward, towards God.'

So the Catholic Church acknowledged the supremacy of conscience?

Absolutely. It has always said that. But in its documents it has usually said 'properly informed conscience', and you will ask what that means. My answer is, one which takes a mature and responsible decision in the light of the various possibilities; and those possibilities must include what the Church herself teaches. But in the last analysis, each of us must be responsible for our own actions before God. The Church can't take that responsibility for us. Even the fact that I was born and brought up a Catholic doesn't mean I have never had to make a real discovery of personal commitment. I don't think faith can become real unless there is a personal commitment made by the individual at an appropriate moment.

So even the Roman Catholic Church does not claim to stand between Christians and their Maker.

Which is not to say that all protests are overruled. Spike Milligan, who regards the Church as 'The hospital of the soul, as much as the hospital is the Church of the body', ripped into the Catholic Church with the dismissal, 'God gave me a mind long before He gave us a Pope.' What is more, Spike doesn't think much of Church unity, either:

Nationalisation of God is not good, any more than nationalisation of the British car industry. I'd rather we diversified. Not that each one hated the other, but acted as a sort of catalyst, saying, 'Look – this is how we're going about being good – are you being good? Fine, that's great, let's be good together.' I love that diversification . . .

Donald Reeves and Neville Black complained from untypically clerical points of view. Reeves, who is incensed by the Church's obsession with its own money and numbers to the exclusion (he thinks) of the Third World and the poor, wants:

A church which is really for everybody, where people can discover their own calling and what it is they are there to do. I'm a great believer in calling out the gifts of people; and that means, in practice, that the oppression the clergy exercise over the people has to be destroyed. I want primarily a lay church, where the clergy help the people to be that church. Almost a reverse of what we've had till very recently. You would have a priest – man or woman – helping people to own their own faith. Then the church would not just be a harmless minority, but a minority which was faithful to its own calling.

Neville Black, of Merseyside, struggles against the built-in class bias of his church. The Church of England, he thinks, has let itself be dominated by middle-class values and as a result has failed in the inner cities.

Working-class people function spontaneously as a gang. But when the gang comes in, it's a threat, and the Church of England has never been able to cope. In this country it has stood on the side of the powerful, the influential and the aspiring individual. We have inner cities impoverished to allow the suburbs to be free. Here in the inner cities the vicious cycle of multi-deprivation is as powerful as ever it was, and we've offered these people no real salvation, no real affirmation, no real redemption or release.

I asked how the Church could offer redemption or release from circumstances that were economic and social? Neville Black said:

By politicising these people in the struggle for a better quality of life. This is what's happening in South America now. We have got to recover that spirit in the inner city. It's a very delicate, sensitive game. It's a tightrope between affirming a sort of Marxism and being authentically Jesus' disciples. Now I'm very definitely not a Marxist; but the Primitive Methodists did get that bit right in the North-east, and I think the South Americans are getting it right today – the connection between politics, culture and Christianity, so that church life becomes an expression of the community.

That may bring a shudder to the Edward Normans of the Church, and sound a far cry from the Body of Christ conjured up by St Paul: 'We, being many, are one body in Christ . . . By one Spirit are we all baptised into one body . . .' But it really stretches the image no further than Paul did. If breath is seen as giving life, if the Spirit is the breath of God and Christians have received that Spirit, then they are a new kind of body, embodying their invisible leader. And a body is not merely to *be* and to pray, but to act. Its members are to care for one another and, as the Church grows and the Day of Judgment fades, for their neighbours. The doctrine of the Incarnation – that God's Word was incorporated in human flesh – has been taken increasingly as meaning that Christians should see His will incorporated in all of human life, and not merely those corners of it reserved to the Church. Again and again I was told: 'Being a Christian is about the whole of life, not just one hour on Sunday morning.'

The corners reserved to the Church were once far more extensive than they are today. Time was when education, the arts, medicine, nursing, even administration were fields of churchly activity. I can see no moral (as distinct from financial) reason why Christians should suppose these fields are barred to them today. As we have already heard, the view that the Church has no place in politics is a comparatively recent heresy.

Bishop Reindorp observed to me:

Politics means the art of living in a city; so when they say the Church is 'getting into' politics, it really is absolute bunk. You're in politics by being alive, by paying rates. I think it's a pity if you become so secularised that you lose the other dimension; but I think that is why I value the privilege that the established bishops have in the House of Lords, of making the voice of the Church heard on problems which, under God, they feel affect the whole nation.

One recalls the interventions of the bishops in the debate over the British Nationality Act.

Of course it is a tightrope walk. Archbishop Derek Worlock sighed: 'When you spell things out, you're accused of politics. If you don't spell them out, you're accused of being an interesting social philosopher . . .' Billy Graham is aware of having spelt things out too specifically in the past: 'If I had my time again, I would be stronger on social injustices and less involved in parties and politics.' Billy, who was close to Richard Nixon and can now only explain the presidential lapses as 'demonic', points out that Jesus did not try to change the Roman Empire and declined to be made King.

But indirectly His followers had a profound effect on the Empire. And throughout church history, Christians have been in the forefront of battles against injustice. But the key is that many issues which are political in nature are also moral and spiritual, so they demand our attention as a church. But I think our primary calling is the proclamation of the gospel. Second is to be servants in whatever political system we find ourselves.

Today, like it or not, the British churches find themselves in a world of anti-colonial, liberation movement politics. Isolationism is tempting, indeed often succumbed to; but as some of my witnesses have noted, the Third World both needs our brotherhood and offers us the brightest examples of vigorous faith in return. Miss Christian Howard (who will forgive me for calling her one of the elder stateswomen of the Church of England) is all too familiar with the resentment some British churchpeople feel towards the World Council of Churches:

I think part of the trouble is that when the churches in Asia, Africa and Latin America came of age, we found it very hard to live on equal terms with people whose particular slant was often quite different to ours. So long as they simply repeated our patterns and ways of doing things, we had no difficulty. They were our daughters or grand-daughters. But the moment they showed that distressing habit of thinking other things more important, it became very difficult for us. What I learnt in Accra in 1974 was that we didn't grasp that the one gospel always comes in some sort of cultural clothing. We were apt to assume that our classic theological way of presenting it was the only possible way. The Africans were saying, 'Whether you are a Roman Catholic or a Protestant, if you are in Africa you tend to have certain ways of looking at it.' And it wasn't only the English who had trouble. I remember one Greek exploding, 'Orthodoxy I know! Catholicism I know! Protestantism I know! But what is this African Church you talk of!' There are some idiotic things done in the World Council, as there are by any of us. But I'm worried by the way we automatically assume that the way *we* judge things is the way everybody else should judge.

But if things are all go in the Third World churches, there is a despondent feeling in many English churches that they have all gone. Bishop Lunn of Sheffield said the main problem affecting his clergy was

a sense of loneliness, isolation, almost uselessness. They won't thank me for saying this, because they work hard, but at this end of the diocese the community as a whole doesn't really feel it needs the Church – any sort of church. I think history has been a little unkind to us: the whole pattern of church life in England is based not on mission, but on the church and the vicar simply being there – like the playing fields and the golf club – for those who happen to be interested. Almost inevitably this has put an undue emphasis on a sort of static stationariness. I wrote a letter the other day to a church warden, thanking him for fifty-four years' service. But a missionary church doesn't have church wardens for fifty-four years!

Even so, I would not want to leave the impression that Bishop Lunn regards his church as a total waste of time:

I think the greatest thing the Church can give is a vision of Jerusalem, a place where people are as God meant them to be, renewed, restored, forgiven, accepted as they are; not at the bottom of the heap, where so many people seem to spend their time. Because they are members of the family of God, very important people. In the life of the local church, there's a vision of excellence. That's why I find myself, as a bishop, going about fussing over the cleanliness and smartness – to show that here is an area where things are done well, with a definite sense of purpose.

Bishop Lunn's remarks bring out two important points

about the Church: the extent to which it has lapsed into folk religion, and the need for the Church both to combat that and to build upon it.

It is common enough to hear of a parish church condemned to closure because nobody uses it, and whose parishoners then fight tooth and nail to keep it open. It has become a symbol without a meaning, yet people will defend the one without the other in a kind of idolatry. Folk religion is full of such disconnections, like the bishop's parish which treats its church as if it were a mere golf club.

John V. Taylor feels very ambivalent about the phenomenon:

One is very aware that folk religion looks in the opposite direction to Christian truth over so many things; and yet I can't dismiss it because it is the one form in which people's instinct for God still finds expression. There's a vestigial belief in God as Fate-with-a-personal-pronoun. There's quite a lot of prayer, and a lot more people read the Bible than ever go to church. A lot has to do with death and our desire for some sort of continuing relationship with people we've loved. One has to include the cult of the cemetery – taking flowers to the grave, visiting cemeteries on Easter afternoon. The necessary increase in cremation is one of those things that is bound to have a profound effect on our folk religion. Again, by secularising the holidays – like Whitsun – we've cut another of the tap roots. The stream of folk religion is weakening rapidly. And yet I find it hard to believe that human beings are going to be permanently reduced to this broken, endlessly mobile individualism knowing nothing at all of community or locality.

So we need the Church – or the churches – to give us community *and* to let us know that our relations with God have more depth to them than we can ever plumb by simply observing the right ceremonies, making the right signs, visiting the right places – and even maintaining a resident holy man called a priest. Paul Bates was only one of my victims who spoke urgently of the need for 'having the local church throw up its own leader'. He did not quite mean the fully qualified, unpaid part-time priest, for he knew of people whose spiritual and pastoral qualities had nothing to do with book-learning. He knew, too, how threatened the clergy could feel by unofficial leadership hiving off some of the best people from their congregations. But, 'We've got to try and find a way of enabling clergy to take on a new role within the community where they are not the sole leader. Their job is to enable that community to throw up its own leadership.'

The ball, then, is in the court of the laity. But does the laity want to play? Increasingly it does. In one West of England parish I met Mrs Broadbent, who had battled her way through the heartbreak of church closure and long interregnums to a magnificent rebirth of village religious life:

People gradually came forward and did something – and it made us. Because there was nobody else to look to, or say 'The vicar should do this, the vicar should do that . . .' we had to do it ourselves. I think it started off socially; there was a spiritual content, but it wasn't very strong. Now we're growing all the time. Since we've had this great and lovely revival we've had a stewardship campaign and we've brought in a lot more money, which means we have to pay a lot more to the parishes that aren't doing so well.

But we are not all lucky enough to live in a ready-made community like an English village, or to belong to a congregation which the Holy Spirit has brought to life. For growing numbers of Christians the only answer is to make a church or a community of their own, whether it is designed to live and work together, or to worship together, or all three. I heard of examples from evangelicals like Graham Cray, from middle-of-the-road Anglicans like John Austen, from radicals like Una Kroll, from Roman Catholics like Rosemary Haughton. Many of them see themselves as reaching back to the original church of the early Christians, and some of them pay little attention to the rules of liturgy and priesthood. Mrs Haughton believes in 'keeping in touch with the Church, but not intimidated by it', saying:

I think it's natural historically that Christianity developed the idea of a separate priesthood, but it's not scriptural and it seems to me we have to rethink that. The early Church didn't have priests in that sense, but the whole people is priestly. The idea of identifying the priesthood as one particular set of people, I find harder and harder to cope with.

Mrs Haughton knows, too, the dangers of a small community becoming authoritarian, even going mad:

The authoritarian thing is one of the easy ways of running a community, but in the end it's extremely destructive. People come together as equals and they want to serve and trust each other. Some of them are learning to make decisions by consensus: it's difficult but essential. It makes a whole difference to the atmosphere in a community.

Una Kroll, who resents the all-maleness of the institutional Church, belongs to a small group that gathers to share bread and wine – sometimes water or an apple – which she finds does need some structure,

some way of fitting into larger groups from time to time, or you can become incestuous, self-sufficient and very complacent. You need a bombshell from the outside, often and often. It's very hard for a small group to open its ranks to other people, so they have to visit the institutions from time to time, discover what's good in them, and perhaps come back and alter. Also such groups have to die occasionally; and it's very painful to know when the time is right to disband and form another.

Austen's groups had not got much further than sharing vegetables, motor-mowers and electric drills, or writing joint letters to MPs. But Cray's were living in extended households,

single folk and marrieds living together under a simple rule of life, thinking very hard about lifestyle and what we spend. But we've made every mistake in the book, and we've come to value the lessons learned by the monastic communities. The grip of materialism is very strong on us and it's much easier to accept the theory than to change the practice. But we genuinely regard one another as brothers and sisters. There's a lot of free giving when extra children come into a small-income family or there's a financial need – often that's met among us voluntarily. The openness to one another, the willingness to share ourselves, our time, our homes – that's different.

Who can say how many Christians will feel able to live this way? I must admit that it goes against my own instinct for privacy and reticence, and that while I admire it, I admire even more those who manage to be Christians *and* everyday, knockabout citizens. I admire Ruth Etchells for saying:

I wish we could dispel the notion that the Church is anything other than a gathering of sinners. If we could catch hold of the fact that most of the people in church have gone there because of some urge for something that's bigger than themselves and will upraise them, not to be made better or to example goodness, then some of the false pictures of the Church would be exploded.

Professor Handy's view was:

The Church is rather like a compost heap. Now the whole point of a compost heap is that after due process of maturing, it should be spread around. And the value of the compost is not judged by the beauty of the heap itself, but by the profusion of the flowers and the quality of the vegetables. The point we must remember about the Church is that its job is to permeate the society in which we live. If it concentrates purely on itself, it will become like a rather interesting compost heap with a few flowers sticking out of the top. How does it spread? By getting out of its churches. The actual institutions of the Church are rather like the fences behind which the compost is collected. The prime duty of Christians is to be at work in all parts of society, not just in offices and factories but in homes and hospitals and schools. I think it was a mistake that the organisation of the Church never changed. At the moment the parish church serves only women, old people and children nearby. It does not minister to able-bodied working men who are in places where the churches don't operate on weekdays.

'On the whole,' said Paul Oestreicher, tolerantly, 'the Church isn't worse than the world around it. It can't pretend to be better and, when it does, other people recognise the hypocrisy of it.'

John Harriott said:

I could sit down and write a book about all the terrible things that the Church has done, and more particularly the people who call

153

themselves members of it. But we confuse the organisational arrangements of the Church with what it is fundamentally about: preserving, maintaining and communicating the very highest ideals of man – telling us what it means to be fully alive – saying, we are not boxed in by space and time.

Personally, I think it does that in a very remarkable way. As one grows older, the more one begins to appreciate this constant irrigation of life not by the cynical, the pessimistic and the hopeless, but by something which is positive, inspiring and enriching. We take it so much for granted. We don't notice how odd it is – that after two thousand years there is such a thing as the Church. It's amazing that it's there at all.

CHAPTER TEN
At Your Service

By popular agreement, more people have been driven out of church by the services than by anything else: 'They're boring, old-fashioned, depressing, unintelligible. Can't understand what's going on.' And yet, wherever you look in the world of the great religions, some sort of service – words or actions or both – seems to be at the heart of it.

Ask a script-writer to bring alive the ancient druids or some primitive tribe, and the chances are he or she will present them chanting a stone-age liturgy and making sacrifices to an idol. It is a form of magic, apparently, and the right thing has to be done in the right way at the right place and time, or the gods will be displeased and things will go badly wrong. That is the essence of folk religion, and it lingers on in various primitive forms of Christianity: even the Bible gets valued not for what it stands for, but for what it objectively is. Get that wrong, and the Devil takes over.

Service, from this point of view, is doing something for God – serving Him – in order to ensure that He will do what we want. At the very least, it should mitigate His anger, which is often unpredictable. That is what many people still believe, deep down inside themselves, and there are traces of it in the Psalms (probably our most ancient liturgical texts) and in parts of the 1662 Prayer Book: 'Like as Thou didst command the destroying Angel to cease from punishing, so it may now please Thee to withdraw from us this plague and grievous sickness . . .' Yet it is profoundly unChristian.

Just as Jesus had little use for the Temple rituals and sacrifices, so Christianity teaches that we are saved not by our own works, not even by holy works done in church, but by grace – by God's undeserved yet freely-given love. After all, what can *we* do for God that would make any difference to Him? If He is as Christians believe Him to be, He certainly deserves our love, attention and praise, but we should not deceive ourselves that He needs it more than we do, or that

155

He will treat us worse if we use the wrong words or forget to cross ourselves at the right moment.

At the same time, as we shall see in the next chapter about sacraments, the developed Christian religion does employ words and actions not for any magical values but for what they express, reveal and teach. These are for us rather than Him, and they come from Him rather than us (a complete reversal of the 'folk' approach). The fact that they come from Him accounts for the desperate efforts the churches have made throughout the ages to get the forms of their services correct. They are meant to be revelations of God, so we had better stick as closely as possible to His intentions as recorded in scripture. At least, that is the starting point.

But since Christians, like Jews, believe in a personal, approachable God, their encounters with Him cannot be *merely* one-way – Him to us. Once again, the key word is 'response'. A Christian service is a conversation with God. It includes not only our love and praise, but our confessions, our troubles, needs and desires. And that is where prayer comes in. At its best prayer, too, is not one-way.

The idea of the service as the worship of the community follows from the Jewish origins. We know that the earliest Christians continued to regard themselves as Jews and to attend the synagogues and the Temple until excluded from them. But it is also clear that, privately, they celebrated the Lord's supper as a meal, during which hymns – probably Psalms – were sung. Within two or three generations, however, something much more formal developed that rose above the setting of a meal. Bread and wine were set apart and consecrated, formulas of words were repeated, and some of those we use today go back to models as early as AD 150. The Eucharist was celebrated on Sundays, which was still an ordinary working day until the fourth century, and the liturgy included readings from various gospels, a teaching sermon, and prayers for the Christian community. Responses, singing, processions, candles and incense, and the recitation of a creed gradually accumulated; while in some local usages the actual consecration of the bread and wine became an elaborate and secret operation, hidden from the common gaze. As Christianity came above ground and moved into imperial surroundings, choirs took over more and more of the role of the congregation and the people became increasingly non-participants. The reformers were reacting against this, among other things, but most of them did not overlook the specific functions of the various portions of the mass.

As a gathering of the community, a service reminds us that Christians are not just a random collection of isolated individuals. This is extremely important, not just because Our Lord created a community and not a philosophy, and ordered its members to love one another, nor because spiritual isolation can become unhealthy, but also because enriching worship does require the dynamics of a group. At the very least, it is more fun.

Or is it? I heard several outbursts against the impertinence of our worship today. Donald Reeves complained that the Church of England's new services were like lectures:

Who the hell wants to go on saying 'We are the Body of Christ' or 'The Lord is here in this'? Endlessly providing information. Who are we doing this for? Certainly not for God. There's a sort of atheism about it. I think a set liturgy is very important, but I think it could have been much, much freer, in a continual state of revision. If you read the discussions about the new Service Book, it's typical white, middle-class, pseudo-intellectual people talking about what's right or wrong. It is not about the way people feel. Some people think liturgy's like saying Beanz meanz Heinz over and over again very beautifully. I don't see that at all.

But perhaps we had better get to grips with the word 'liturgy' itself. Dean Jasper of York, who was largely responsible for the services Donald Reeves dislikes so much, explained that in classical Greece 'liturgy' was used to describe a person's individual contribution to some corporate state enterprise: perhaps a ship and its crew contributed towards the fleet – that was a liturgy. St Paul used the same word to describe a group of Christians helping a less fortunate group with money. 'And you get this dual thing of both menward and Godward activities, they are all liturgies. It's not badly translated by the word *service*.'

157

Professor Handy agrees that all religions have found the repetition of rituals helpful.

It does help somehow to distance oneself from the clutter of the world and get into one's inner core, which is where I think God is. Worship, I think, is helping to put me in touch with the God who is in me and also in everybody else; which is why worship has to be corporate. Jung talked about the collective unconscious; I like to think about the collective God somehow belonging in all of us. But I find highly participatory, innovative liturgies very distracting, because I am concentrating so much on what I am supposed to do next – whether I am meant to rush out and hug somebody or hold something – that I don't tune in to the eternal mysteries and verities.

Professor Handy is fortunate to live and work next door to St George's Chapel, Windsor, where the ceremonies have hardly changed since 1348. 'While that irritates many, it pleases me mightily. Particularly when it's accompanied by a great deal of beautiful singing, all of which helps to tune me into myself and to the God within me.'

That kind of Anglicanism has changed less than the Roman Catholicism it replaced. Father Jock Dalrymple, a Scots Catholic, remarked that the words 'liturgical worship' conjured up a rather sticky following of forms:

In my own church we have got less ossified in our ritual as compared with twenty years ago, and my time as a priest is much more informal and therefore more real. But you still have to have guidelines. Mankind is intensely communal; anything good you want to share. Ritual comes from handing on good things to the next generation.

I had a long talk about liturgy with Dom Edmund Jones, who heads a small Roman Catholic community of monks and nuns. Liturgical language, he thought, should be highly poetical and allusive rather than intellectually verbal. 'The liturgy is a work of art, a sort of sacred dance going on in highly stylised movements. And if it's living, it does something to people.'

Dom Edmund thought the Catholics' changeover from Latin to English had been made too much of.

There has been much more revolutionary change than that in the course of the Church's history. We used to have sinners making public confession, with a long public penance following. When they switched in the tenth century to private confession, with penance done after you had been absolved and readmitted to communion – that was an enormous upheaval. From Latin to English is a mini-change compared to that.

We were talking about the mass, which is essentially what non-Romans would call a communion service or the Lord's supper. But what about the sermon or homily, the preaching of the Word to which Protestants attach so much importance?

Father Dalrymple, with his neighbours of the Church of Scotland in mind, said he viewed this with some suspicion.

Too much emphasis on Word and not so much on mystical sacramental worship can lead to a very conceptualised version of Christianity. There's a poem by Edwin Muir, talking of the Calvinist preachers of his youth up in Orkney, where he says, 'The Word made flesh is here made word again.' And I think a lot of worship in our sister church is very wordy. That's because they have depressed symbolism.

Here, of course, is one of the basic points of disagreement between Protestant and Catholic. Whatever political wedges may have been used to force the gap wider, there remain two broad theologies, one emphasising the supremacy of Bible-based teaching from the pulpit, the other the supremacy of the sacramental activity at the altar. Supporting the basic division there are subsidiary ones, notably over the role and authority of the ministry or priesthood – though it has to be said that in extreme cases there has not been much to choose between Catholic clerical tyranny and Protestant clerical tyranny. I have noticed, however, during my interviews, a much greater emphasis on preaching among the Romans and a much greater emphasis upon the sacraments among the Protestants than I would have found twenty or thirty years ago. As a significant accompaniment to this, Catholic theology and Protestant spirituality have both come alive.

Churches in the Reformed tradition still tend to make less use of sacraments and more of the Word than do those of a Catholic persuasion. But before the Reformation even Catholics communicated very seldom. In the view of the reformers, a non-communicating mass was wrong; if there was mass, there ought to be communion. Calvin, indeed, tried to insist upon communion every Sunday, and was only defeated by the people, who were not accustomed to it. So was developed what was known as 'the dry Mass', a form of service which stopped short of the actual communion and became the origin of the non-sacramental service which has become the custom in Protestantism but originally arose through a failure to accomplish what the reformers intended.

Archbishop Runcie says Anglicans rather pride themselves on having tried to get the balance right between emphasis on the sacrament, which without preaching can degenerate into superstition, and emphasis on the Word, which without communion can underestimate the presence of the Lord in the midst of His people.

The early church was undivided on the matter of the Eucharist. It was only in the Middle Ages that the sacrament tended to become a thing in itself. And in the over-emphasis of the pulpit and the reading desk you get a break-up of the original unity of word and sacrament. Of course some Anglicans emphasise the Catholic tradition and some the Protestant. But the fundamental commitment in our Prayer Book is to a very close unity of the two.

Dom Edmund Jones told me the official Catholic line was that the sermon (or homily) was:

very much part of the breaking of the bread of the Word to the people. It is an integral part of the liturgy – though whether that is always observed is another matter. St Caesarius of Arles has a marvellous line: 'If we take care that no fragment of the Body should fall to the ground through our negligence, we should take equal care that nothing of the Word should fall unheeded.' That is the authentic Catholic position. St Caesarius goes on to speak of the clergy as *cows* – rather strange ones with only two teats, the Old Testament and the New – and he says that if they are slack about giving this nourishment to the people, then the people should be like calves coming up to them and kneading away at them till they force the milk out of them.

Traditionally, the Word in services involves the reading and expounding of scripture. From that point of view the Bible is largely a liturgical text to be read out at worshipful gatherings, not a history book for private study. The Book of Psalms is the original hymn book and, I would say, the mightiest of all books of prayer. But, as we have heard, the Bible's significance for us is not always straightforward, and an ingenious preacher can pick and choose his texts to suit his preconceptions; which is one reason for sympathising with Jock Dalrymple's reservations.

Dean Eric Heaton of Christ Church, Oxford, insists:

The Old Testament was not written to be read in patches four inches long, by someone standing behind a brass duck in an Oxford hood. I suppose you can read the Prophet Amos, passionately and vehemently, in about twenty minutes. But the power of it can't be contained in a liturgical context, with the Magnificat right after it. Of course there are some great passages that *can* be used in a service: any of Isaiah 40 and 55 is suitable material for reading in short lessons. But the Old Testament is being used now under the impress of so-called biblical theology – an attempt to make the outstanding themes of the Bible into something like systematic theology and impose it on the material out of context. Sometimes I call it 'shish-kebab theology', because you get a great skewer and collect these passages on it, like pieces of lamb, tomato and onion, and then you wave it around and say, 'This is doctrine.' I'm being rather severe, but a lot of the lessons are bent towards some correspondence with the New Testament, and that means the Old is not allowed to say its own thing in its own terms.

Dean Heaton was the scholar who thought the Christian layman would do better to stick to the New Testament and not worry his head about the Old, though 'One would be terribly distressed if the psalter lost its place in Christian spirituality. But the use of the psalter is not really an intellectual one. It's meditative and therefore rather special.'

There are, of course, all styles of service; from the total silence of a Quaker Meeting to the ecstasies of Pentecostalism, by way of the ritual dance of the mass, the scholarly exposition of the Kirk and the hymn recitals punctuated by extempore prayer of certain nonconformists. The Eastern Orthodox offers us a glimpse of Heaven, some of the American fundamentalists I have attended seemed more concerned to keep us in line by threatening us with communist hell-fire.

Does God need to be worshipped, in any of these ways? Dom Edmund answers: 'He has the *right* to be worshipped, but I don't think He needs it. We need to express our relationship with Him, and it's wrong if we don't.' But would God be worse off if we did not worship Him? (I was thinking here of William Vanstone's theory of love rejected and incomplete.)

'I never quite know the answer to this one. How much God suffers is a great mystery to me. I honestly don't know. But *we* would be worse off, that's for sure.'

However, there are those who deny that; who claim they don't need to go to church but find Him very deeply in music or on country walks. David Isitt says churchgoing doesn't deny any of those experiences, though whether having experiences is what worship is about is more questionable.

I go to church very often indeed, and I have long since stopped expecting to have particular experiences as though it were some kind of fruit machine: a lot of people think that's what worship is. I do occasionally get a tingle up the spine from the music – not often from the sermon – but the act of public worship is really a matter of engaging yourself with your fellow Christians and – I would be old-fashioned enough to say – carrying out certain duties. That goes way back to the Old Testament: 'Thou shalt love the Lord thy God and thou shalt worship Him.' This seems to me to be some kind of imperative laid on the believer: not to try and go it alone, not to despise those with whom he is called, but to participate with them in a common act.

There were not many who spoke so categorically of a duty to serve. Rather more were aware of the Church's duty to cater for its congregations. Stuart Miller, the Scottish religious broadcaster, contrasted his duty to be interesting and even entertaining with the Church's neglect of those qualities:

In a pulpit, you've got a captive audience that you don't need to entertain. On the whole, the churches are very, very boring, the music is centuries out of date, the language of the hymns is incomprehensible. A radio programme is forced to speak the language of the man in the street. A bit of competition between the radio programme and the Church doesn't worry me at all. I simply hope it will teach the Church the lesson that it will have to update its music and its language and go in for entertainment. If a sermon isn't interesting and entertaining it won't communicate. I've been at the centre of a debate in the Church of Scotland magazine, for suggesting the music should be radically altered. I'm not opposed to those who would like to retain the traditional style. But I think they are a minority clique and I think they should do it in their own minority time. If the Church is involved in Mission, then it's going to have to speak the language of the people round it.

Neville Black learnt the Prayer Book by heart in Bootle, when he was a kid,

And people who've learnt it then want to impose it on today's generation. But that isn't the way. And I'm not very happy with the Alternative Service Book. It's too massive and too literary. I want liturgy and faith to be built around residual symbols: communion to me is bread, wine, fellowship and celebration. If Bach turns you on or, as some of my friends do, singing plainsong, have it! But if we take off having a Eucharist in a pub, when people are slightly bevvied, then that's where it's got to start. But you see, the Church of England is in the stranglehold of the Home Counties mentality. I'd want to break that.

I can imagine that a public bar Eucharist might express a great deal of fellowship, but would it teach what the Church claims to have had handed down to it: since one of the aims of a set liturgy is just that, to teach? We are back once more to the point of protecting doctrine, inadequate though it may be, sooner than letting it be drowned by the world's natural uproar.

Probably nothing does more to frame the Briton's theology than the particular hymn book used; though perhaps it is more important to say it frames his, and her, emotional attitude to religion: either sturdily four-square (as in a metrical psalm), sunnily optimistic (as in a salvationist hymn), or stickily sentimental (as in one of the Victorian favourites). Music can be a great trap in church: if the congregation sings badly, it can ruin the whole service; if it sings too well, the service becomes a concert; if the choir takes over, the congregation might just as well not be there. People like Stuart Miller complain about antiquated music, but if you try to bring the music up to date there are laments about the dear old favourites.

Caryl Micklem would like to throw out what he calls:

the cushions, the mindless expressions of repose in the Lord and joy in thoughts of Heaven. There were cries of outrage among the Methodists when they threatened not to put 'Blessed Assurance' in their new book. I don't want the Church to be uncomfortable for discomfort's sake, and I certainly don't want it joyless. What I dislike is mindlessness. I want the joy that people express to be something that really emerges from their thinking as well as their feeling. I distrust hymns that simply play on feeling. I worry a lot about singing very personal hymns like Wesley's 'And Can It Be?' to the traditional tune, which turns this intensely inward thing into some kind of rant. It amazes me that people can sing it in that way, and I can't feel it does anybody any good to do so.

There is, I suppose, a twofold link between worship and the arts: first that art has always been used to honour and beautify the palace of the king, and second that artists are a kind of prophet, telling things like they are. This last function may be disturbing, for it means that a true hymn or carving or window may not necessarily be a pretty one. Edward Robinson, who has spent many years at Oxford researching religious experience, told me:

Beauty so often is used to describe experiences which are merely comfortable or pleasant or satisfying, and a great deal of religious experience is none of those. It's often very shocking.

I'm sure that a religion which is not in touch with the contemporary arts of its culture is on the way out. And that is why I feel very depressed indeed about the relationship today. The drifting apart has been happening for centuries. Certainly for the last three hundred years in Western Europe there has been no explicitly religious art of any value. I'm not really concerned with finding the historical causes for this, so much as trying to build bridges between artists who are attempting to express profoundly spiritual insights into life – between them and the ecclesiastical establishment.

Dean Tony Bridge of Guildford is presumably part of that establishment, though he takes a less sympathetic view of what modern *musicians* are up to:

I tend to agree with one of the reactionary Popes, that all religious music stopped in about 1400. I'm not really in favour of strumming guitars and throbbing drums: I don't think this is music which speaks a religious language, it speaks the language of human courtship. Great fun, social amusement, but it isn't a patch on the Negro spirituals, which were genuinely religious music. When we write a folk mass we really don't do anything of the kind – we write some dreary pastiche.

The Orthodox, the most unchanging and traditional of all the Christian families, would never dream of such a thing. They trace their liturgy back to St John Chrysostom in the fourth century. And yet they claim to be closest of all to their people. Says Metropolitan Anthony:

I think that the difference between East and West is that the clergy in the West were a cultural elite. They never were with us. The Orthodox was a popular church, the heart of which was worship. It was a great deal simpler and less touched by various philosophies succeeding each other.

You cannot attend an Orthodox service without being struck by the attention that is given to the icons: those formalised paintings of saints which at first sight appear to be worshipped to idolatry. Metropolitan Anthony is always having to correct that impression:

The treatment that we give them in terms of veneration is not very different from the way in which a person treats the photograph of someone he loves deeply. There is not any sense in which it is a relic in itself or an object of worship. But although it is not the person, it is close to expressing the person. The formula is that the veneration we pay to the icon is addressed to its prototype. We look, as it were, through the icon as one can look through a stained-glass window at the beauty of the radiance of the light on the other side.

Commonly the icon, like the crucifix hanging on a bedroom wall, becomes the focus of prayer; and it is time we looked at this mode of worship. What, then, is prayer?

Dom Edmund Jones once knew a woman in her mid-thirties who still began her bed-time prayers, 'Gentle Jesus, meek and mild . . .' 'She had got a long way to go towards what understanding what prayer is about,' sighed Dom Edmund.

I find it most difficult to justify interceding with God for various requests. To me, the most obvious word is *adoration*.

I maintain that people pray a great deal more than they think. Any reaction of wonderment is already on the path of prayer. There's a couple of gasometers on the North Circular Road in London – lovely things with beautiful lace-work round the top – and when I go past them, my heart always leaps with joy at seeing them. That, I believe, is prayer – this reaction of wonderment. I remember talking about this to someone who was having a problem with prayer, and she said: 'Oh, I'm so relieved, because all the way here on the bus I kept thinking what a beautiful day it was.' Well, this was prayer, in fact, at an early stage. Certainly if she had added, 'Thank you God,' it would have been very much prayer. But the fact that people react wonderingly and gratefully to things is the beginning of prayer.

Was Dom Edmund persuaded that things happened which would not have happened without prayer? 'The only answer I can give is that I know of things that have happened to my surprise after prayer.' Was he sure that in some sense prayer was answered? 'Oh yes, I'm sure of that. Often the answer is not the one we were expecting. Often it is very much more than we wanted.'

Like Dom Edmund, I am bothered by prayers of intercession. Surely God will know best, if He has not decided already what we should have? Is not intercessory prayer going back to a kind of magical approach; to a belief that we can manipulate God if only we use the right words?

Peter Baelz thinks it is perfectly natural:

I don't believe that desires are things to be suppressed. They are things to be purified and redirected. Telling God what I want is like throwing the wand into the pool of Divinity and seeing what happens to it.

The gospels certainly tell us: 'What things soever ye desire, when ye pray, believe that ye receive them, and ye shall have them.' But what about the opposite sides in a battle, each praying for victory? Margaret Bowker does not believe that they should. 'I believe each should be praying that the will of God be done – which is Christ's prayer – and should be praying for the state of humanity and for all who are suffering and dying, whatever their side.'

Or a woman praying for money for her Spanish holiday?

If through that she also became aware that prayer is a means of love, by which you could ask for things for your neighbour, the unemployed, the prisoner – I'm sure God would say, Well done! But if she really thinks God is going to give her money for a Spanish holiday when there are so many people dying of starvation, then I don't think she's got very far with prayer. It's got to be two-way – listening more and more after the necessary petition for others. It has got to move more and more into a deep silence of listening and becoming aware of the order of priorities: which certainly doesn't exist in our society as we have it at the moment.

The Lord's Prayer, the very pattern of Christian worship, divides our response to God into two halves: first, adoration and acknowledgment of His glory and authority; second, our petitions for bread, forgiveness and protection. But (which is Margaret Bowker's point) it is *our* daily bread, mankind's and not just my own; and as Jesus emphasises in the eleventh chapter of St Mark, God's forgiving us depends upon our forgiving others.

167

Margaret Bowker's emphasis upon the listening side of prayer naturally appealed to my Quaker instincts. The more silence, the better as far as my worship is concerned (though one has to be careful it does not exclude all sense of praise and joy). Quakers have a saying that 'the silence brings unity', by which they mean not just a mutual telepathic togetherness but that – given the chance – something new, unexpected and immensely valuable may enter the meeting and bring together different strains of thought. In psychological terms you might call it 'lateral thinking'. On the religious level, Kenneth Barnes calls it 'an experience of transcendence – the transcendent activity of the inner light or Holy Spirit'.

I had not expected to find much common cause between Quakerism and Catholicism, but I did when I talked to Timothy Wright at Ampleforth. He said:

It seems to me that the practice of prayer touches a deep level within me where – this sounds very presumptuous – I find God. But this is a momentary experience. More often than not there is a darkening, and a need to persevere without much clue except that general direction. I think when one talks of prayer one has got to talk in terms of silence, discipline and darkness, rather than of emotional satisfaction, elation, joy, praise – which is much more of the charismatic variety.

Too often people are taught that prayer is reciting formulae together. Many people fall away from prayer because it has ceased to have any meaning for them. In my experience, the starting point is not words but silence. It is only when one creates a space for stillness that one can become aware of something deeper. Teaching people to pray, you don't put a prayer book in their hands, you put them in a room on a chair and tell them to sit still for ten minutes. If persevered with, it produces on one level a calmness, and on another the realisation that there is a deeper level of consciousness than the emotional, imaginative side of one; and as you penetrate that deeper level, that is where you can encounter God.

Perhaps the most extraordinary instance of this that I recorded came from Father Jock Dalrymple, who 'as a rather traditional-minded chap' had his entire attitude to the Vatican Two changes transformed by an experience in prayer.

What was the experience like? I asked. 'Just of God,' said Jock Dalrymple.

For about twenty minutes I just knew that God was more real than anything else, and that He wasn't 'out there' but that He permeated me – that He and I occupied the same space, and He was real. It altered my whole attitude to Vatican Two and authority in the Church and to my priesthood.

All of which makes prayer sound a rather lonely and awful thing, with the soul almost speechless before its maker. One of my Scottish Presbyterian victims, Professor Shaw, agreed that prayer was indeed a matter of opening oneself and listening,

but also of talking. I have difficulty with some modern interpretations of prayer which think that to talk is to adopt a very anthropomorphic or man-centred view of God. If God is love, as I believe Him to be, then I have no alternative but to make my requests known to Him and try to see prayer as an instrument of compassion. So I don't think one should fight shy of prayer as a talking as well as a listening.

So it appears that worship and prayer are inseparable, and two-way. In worship, God communicates with us and we with Him; in prayer it is the same. Both involve talking and listening. Both involve adoration and petition. And both can involve darkness and struggle, as well as light and joy. They can even, as some of the Psalms illustrate, involve protest. Valerie Fisher described a hilarious dialogue with the Almighty over a particularly dreadful school class:

So I went to the church just opposite and said, 'Right, you lot, you've made a flippin' awful job of it so far this term, just you plan this next lesson.' So I planned that lesson in church, full of fury, and it was just as bad. So I would go back in and say, 'Look God, that was as bad as ever.' I was that wild, you know . . .

'And what answer did you get?' I enquired.

'I've had two thousand years of successes and failures – you've only just started.'

Ruth Etchell's dialogue was less in the style of Don Camillo. Her clergyman father had been a delightful and humble man, a faithful servant of his Lord,

and though I did not respect his intellectual capacity or agree with his faith, I did respect his faithfulness. So when he had a stroke and was robbed of any mental qualities at all and became like a three-year-old, I had to come to grips with the question of whether he had been living with a total delusion all his life, or whether in fact the Lord he had been preaching was much bigger than the one I had rejected in listening to him. This was no longer intellectual theory – this was the very stuff of life.

Had it never occurred to her, as it had to the psalmist, that God often seems to be unjust to his people, and that there is a good case for protest?

Yes, indeed. But before one can protest one must have a passionate conviction about the kind of God one is protesting to. If He is a God to whom justice means nothing, there is no point in making an issue of it. It's only if you passionately believe that He is the God of justice that, in your rage, you can say what you think to Him – as I frequently did when I stood alongside my father's bed. One could because one believed there was a justice, not in that figure there, but in God – a God who has entered human life and has taken it over. Then you feel safe enough to hammer Him, because He knows what it is about.

CHAPTER ELEVEN

Bread, Water and Wine

'I know mumbo-jumbo when I hear it,' I told my school chaplain, 'And your services are pure witchcraft!' I must admit that deep down in my protestant twentieth-century soul there is still a part of me that feels the same, that knows that bread and wine are not the body and blood of Jesus (how disgusting if they were!) and that wants to shout 'Rubbish!' when the vicar declares that marriage signifies 'the mystical union that is betwixt Christ and His Church'.

Sacraments have always bothered me enormously and still do, for I belong to a church – the Society of Friends – which does not employ sacraments or a priesthood to administer them. No baptism, no confirmation, no communion, and we marry ourselves. Though it is arguable that members of the Society do in fact have a profoundly sacramental approach to life, for more than three centuries they have survived without framing it in special occasions. I am not advocating this for everyone. It has not exactly spread like wildfire, in any case, and most Christians would argue that there are very specific instructions from Our Lord to observe His Supper, the Eucharist, the Holy Communion. It is an observance that the Church seems to have kept from the very beginning.

The basic reason for Quakers abandoning the practice was that in their eyes, by the mid-seventeenth century, the sacraments had become an empty performance not reflecting any integrity of conduct. Today some Quakers do receive communion from ordained ministers of other churches; and a Friend like Kenneth Barnes, married to a Roman Catholic, would like to see Quakers in closer touch with the sacramental churches and making more of church festivals such as Christmas and Easter. Friends are also much less anti-clerical than they used to be.

The Salvation Army does not use sacraments, either. Like Quakers, they feel that anything which tries to imprison the Holy Spirit within forms needs to be challenged. But originally their abstention was the result of a mixture of motives: it avoided disputes over what type of communion the new church should adopt, and whether women should be permitted to administer it; it removed the alcoholic temptations of wine; and it emphasised the persistent evangelical doctrine, that God could change a person's life without reference to anything but the faith in his own heart.

Major Kenneth Howe, like the other Salvationists I spoke to, insisted that he did not feel deprived by declining the sacraments.

Where we may miss something is in terms of association with fellow Christians; but in my experience there are other opportunities. Still, any group which is non-sacramental lays itself open to a much greater responsibility in this area, in that the whole of life must be seen as sacramental.

Something sacramental is sacred. It is the outward and visible sign of something inward and spiritual. So that to say the whole of life is sacramental – a phrase much used by Quakers, too – is to say something very far-reaching that should alter one's whole approach to life and abolish any distinction between experience and religious experience. For it implies that everything we encounter is not a mere object, but sign of God's grace. This is sometimes hard to remember, when waiting for a train in the Underground or unstopping a blocked sewer; but is it harder to believe than that His will is expressed in a morsel of bread and a sip of wine?

Another Salvationist, Ken Lawson, said:

The important thing is that I do not forget the dying of Lord Jesus, the broken body and shed blood. When reformers like Zwingli said the sacrament was a memorial meal, it was only a matter of time before somebody said, 'Well, we can remember without having these physical elements here.' Perhaps we are in that line of descent. The fact that we don't have the constant reminder of the physical elements could make us fail to remember as powerfully as we ought to; but it is equally possible to go through the mechanical exercise of receiving the bread and wine without thinking what they mean. Both sides have their value for people with that kind of faith.

But the sacrament of the Eucharist does have immense significance for the majority of practising Christians, whatever their denomination. Michael Taylor, the eminent Baptist, spoke of 'all sorts of overtones', adding:

I don't want to be the kind of Zwinglian Baptist who says the only thing he's doing is remembering Jesus. For me, there are allusions to a whole number of meals: the meals Jesus ate with His disciples, the meals in the wilderness, the meal in the upper room, the meal with the risen Christ by the lakeside, the meals that were shared by the early Christian communities, and the promise of that splendid meal when the creative activity of God moves on. But if Christ is present in human life, He is present all the time. I don't understand the talk about the presence of Christ in the Eucharist if it means he is present there and not everywhere else.

John Harriott, the Roman Catholic, said too:

It's all sorts of things, from the Old Testament. It looks back to the covenant between God and Abraham. It looks back to the liberation from Egypt and the thanksgiving they offered. And it looks back to the sacrifices of the Old Testament. It is *the* sacrifice, of somebody who could stand in the presence of God and Father representing the whole of humanity throughout time. It is a meal, too, but a meal in which we actually eat God. That's terribly pagan-sounding – it's not cannibalism – but we are reunited with God in the act of eating what appear to be bread and wine and have, by an act of God Himself, been made the body and blood of Christ in a certain way. I also think it's the act through which the Church expresses its nature and through which the whole community comes together and becomes visible.

At this point, the voice of Methodist Lord Soper breaks through in my mind, asserting 'Do this in remembrance of me', and complaining about 'the attempt to prescribe certain interpretations.' He went on:

What has bothered me is the way in which this fundamentally central fact of remembrance has been cluttered up with all kinds of ideas and commitments which are exclusive and have caused any amount of trouble between the churches, which might have remained together if they hadn't become too obsessed with them.

It sounded to me as if Cardinal Hume's church was being accused of doing the cluttering. Father Basil thought for a bit, then remarked: 'I don't think there were any real problems in the theology of the Eucharist until the tenth century. It was extraordinary how long it survived without question.' But why would not Roman Catholics share the Eucharist with members of other churches?

The view has always been that the Eucharist should be the expression of unity, not the means to achieve it. Eucharist and Church are terms which explain each other. We feel it's important that we should have the same faith as to what the Eucharist is. I believe it is truly the body and blood of Jesus Christ, and if my neighbour does not believe this, then we are not one in our faith. This seems to us important.

Archbishop Runcie offered an Anglican compromise:

We've allowed a considerable degree of agnosticism about definitions within the Eucharist. Wasn't it Queen Elizabeth who started that jingle?

> *Christ was the Word, He spake it,*
> *And what His Word doth make it,*
> *That I believe and take it.*

Anglicans would probably want something a little more objective than what Lord Soper has suggested, and something a little less tightly defined than what Cardinal Hume has said.

Francis Glasson declared solidly:

I believe that when I take that piece of bread and it becomes part of my frame, it is woven into my nerves and muscles, so that as I do that in faith I receive Jesus Christ, the Bread of Life, who strengthens me and passes into my being; so that I can say, 'I live, yet no longer I, but Christ liveth in me.' And I believe that the sacrament is a vehicle of divine grace and – receiving it in faith and humility and penitence – that new life comes into me.

Paul Oestreicher said:

Here is ordinary bread, ordinary wine, transformed into something with eternal significance. The body and blood significance can be overdone. But the repetition of this act of God sharing Himself with His people, in a communal act that makes us one with Him, is to me deeply personal and also radically political.

Political? How so?

If God is our brother and shares His life with each of us, this commits us to one another; and that commitment is not just to those who chose to receive communion, but to all who are invited – and that means the whole family of man. The corporate significance of this sacrament is even greater than its individual meaning. It makes us all equal in a very profound sense.

Round the table of a Sabbath, Jewish families regularly celebrate what might appear to be a Eucharist, with the sharing of unleavened bread and wine. 'But it is not a sacrament,' insisted Rabbi Gryn, 'the wine continues to be wine and the bread remains bread. And the message of our Passover meal is really about human liberty.'

My Jewish friends continued to disbelieve that Jesus the Jew could have meant what Christians say He meant. Rabbi Blue insisted:

The whole force of Judaism is to disassociate itself from mythological elements: they were the bane of the old Hebrew life. The idea of eating one's God and using blood in relation to wine would be enough to make a Jew faint, if he took the idea seriously.

Moslems have nothing equivalent to a sacrament, though Gai Eaton thought there might be an abstract parallel in the opening verses of the Koran, used by every Moslem to validate his prayers:

I don't see why we should not say that just as the Christian absorbs the sacramental bread into himself, so the Moslem eats these sacred words. 'Eats' may seem odd, yet I think it is appropriate because it is one of our aims to incorporate the sacred words into our very substance.

The idea of making God part of oneself is not so pagan when you think how opposed to idolatry Moslems are.

But did Christ really institute and authorise the sacraments? For a start, Roman Catholics recognise seven (baptism, confirmation, Eucharist, penance, sacrament of the sick, holy orders and matrimony), whereas most Protestants recognise only baptism and holy communion as being ordained by God. The Thirty-nine Articles declare the remainder are 'grown partly of the corrupt following of the Apostles, partly are states of life allowed in the Scriptures, but yet have not like nature . . .' At the other extreme we have seen how, to some Christians, almost anything may convey God to us and thus be called *sacramental*. But such Christians would deny that those experiences had to be ministered to us by the Church, which is an important element in Catholic theory. It will not quite do to say we are all sacramentalists now.

Catholics regard the Church as the fundamental sacrament through which all others are communicated. Some Protestants tend to view this suspiciously as a means of reserving power to Rome and its priesthood, of keeping the laity in subservience. Catholics will argue that such authority is justified in scripture where Christ entrusts his ministry to the apostles; and Protestants may reply that scripture – as in Chapter 23 of Matthew – forbids a churchly hierarchy and gives no basis for much of Catholic sacramental theology. There is no easy way out of the difference. We can only regard the two approaches as different ways up the same mountain.

In order to come to grips with the deepest significance of the sacraments, I have chosen to confine myself almost entirely to the holy communion. I agree this is a pity, for it would have been fun to examine confession (with its modern psychiatric implications and its hint of the Church as Big Brother), baptism (with its misleading folk religion overtones of washing out the Devil) and marriage (always ambivalently viewed by the Church, and only appropriated as a true sacrament in 1439). It was Jack Dominian who pointed out that the essentials of Christian marriage – life-long commitment, exclusiveness, fidelity, life-giving and love – make up an accurate sign of God's relationship with man. Dr Dominian added:

I think Christianity is absolutely right in insisting upon a public ceremony, for two reasons. Marriage is both a public and a private event, but if we make it entirely private, marriage will suffer in the long run because the community has to support it. Secondly, as the Church learnt five hundred years ago, there is a grave danger that without this public covenant, people will promise themselves to more than one person, there will be much confusion about who belongs to whom, and a lot of harm will be done. A public ceremony elicits the support of the community and adds a commitment to work hard at the problem of marital survival.

I should have been glad to spend longer on this, and on whether the Church was really right to elevate marriage into a sacrament. But another problem calls.

When Cardinal Hume remarked 'Eucharist and the Church are terms which explain each other', he might equally have said 'Sacraments and the Church'. In Catholicism, sacraments are what the Church is for and what it is about. By insisting that matter – the bread, water and wine – can reflect a mysterious spiritual reality, the Church found its answer to the tempting oriental heresy known as Gnosticism, that matter is evil. The Catholic Church prefers to describe sacraments as *signs* rather than *symbols*, but the two are not far apart; and as so much art is symbolic – material signs evoking inner meanings – sacramentalism has also helped to give the Church a certain aesthetic quality. Which accounts for the fact that, of all religions, none has had a closer alliance with the arts than Christianity: for they are essentially sacramental.

Sacraments are spoken of as *mediating* God to man, and in Catholic theology it is the Church that acts as the mediator. Certainly the Church protects doctrine, but it would be wrong to think of the Church as being solely the priesthood: it is the entire People of God. In this it is helping to guard against an atomised, individualistic Christianity, only concerned with personal salvation. The Church is seeking to maintain a solidarity of mankind, even a solidarity of sin, which is not out of keeping with modern social and political philosophy.

The more emphatic Protestant will resist the attempt to place an institutional mediator between himself and God, for he will see in this the danger of substituting works – mere actions – for faith; and he will resent the Catholic claim that sacraments are acts of the Church, expressions of its nature and mission, besides being channels of divine grace. The Protestant will want to see them as coming directly from God. He might argue – but probably will not – that it is as shaky to say that Jesus instituted the sacraments as to say that he founded the Church. In a sense Jesus was responsible for both, and neither would have existed without the other. But it is ridiculous to argue that He dictated the rules and regulations for either. What we have now, in various churches, is descended from what was devised by people very much closer to Jesus and His intentions than we are.

But did they go wrong somewhere? Did they truly follow Christ's intentions as far as we can check them in the gospels? Concentrating on the sacrament of holy communion, it is debatable what the gospels really show us in the last supper. If we had only Matthew and Mark, we might see in them a prophetic gesture of resignation – Jesus, unable to eat or drink, passing his abandoned portion to the others – but no deliberate creation of a ceremony; while John, throughout the long farewell discourse attributed to Our Lord, does not even break bread or bless the cup, besides putting the supper at least a day earlier than the others. Only Luke, in a single phrase which is repeated and developed later by St Paul, suggests that Jesus wanted His followers to copy His actions.

(Incidentally, I have never been able to understand why the washing of the feet, so obviously commended as a ceremony in John's gospel, has not been faithfully observed by the Church, or only very feebly on Maunday Thursdays. As a sacrament of service it would do the clergy a power of good; though I suppose it would be messy.)

It does not follow, however, that the Lord's supper is a bogus invention, though it has obviously been heightened and ritualised. John's Chapter 6 makes it clear that he is perfectly familiar with the idea that Christians should 'eat the flesh of the Son of man and drink His blood'.

And it is quite natural that Jesus' followers should have celebrated His memory and His continuing presence in a meal. In the East, a shared meal is still a sign of community and peace. Jesus Himself spread His good news by sharing meals with sinners and social outcasts, quite apart from the special significance He may have attached to that final supper with His friends.

It seems to me that those who resist sacramentalism might ask themselves why it is that most Christians have always felt the need to *do* something in this way, rather than merely contemplate the Lord. When I asked Professor Dennis Nineham what he thought was happening in the Eucharist, he replied that it was far too big a subject for him to answer briefly without being misunderstood.

But any clergyman would agree that one of the most moving experiences in one's life is to administer the bread and the wine to people. Whatever else it brings them, you can see that it brings them comfort and strength.

Stuart Blanch agreed:

When I walk along the altar rail, distributing the bread of life, at that moment I really feel this is what it's all about. I feel as though I am back on the mountainside in Galilee with the disciples, going amongst the crowd with their baskets of bread.

I do not have any theory, thank God – I do not have to defend it, therefore – as to how the bread can become spiritual food. I think my own view of the Eucharist is entirely controlled by that experience of the people of God gathered round Christ and His disciples at the feeding of the five thousand.

We have encountered information theory already in this book; Paul Fueter is an expert on it working for the Bible Society. He told me:

What you do as a radio person is a fleeting experience – something that just goes by. Really to influence people, they need something more: something they can touch, they can read, after the event has taken place.

This role of the tangible token is very important. We live with it

179

all the time. The photographs we put in our albums after our holidays function in this way. And in Christian communication we also need the tangible token. The whole Bible is full of them, beginning with the rainbow after Noah's Ark. Every time you look at this rainbow you'll remember, 'I will have mercy on My people.' The Old Testament was the tangible token used by Jesus all the time – the scriptures were tangible, they were in the synagogues and people kept little bits of them in their homes – so Jesus used them with His disciples to explain His resurrection: He had to say, 'It's all written in the scriptures.' And now the New Testament functions in the same way.

You will see that we can talk of the sacraments like that, too. The bread and the wine are tangible tokens of Christ's real coming into the world, His body being broken and His blood shed. According to your churchmanship you will have different interpretations of how this is meant; but the important thing is that they are tangible tokens of the great events of Crucifixion and Resurrection. The element of remembrance is there, too, and of understanding and of announcing the gospel.

Two Roman Catholics join in. Says Jock Dalrymple:

Symbols are ways of saying things not using words, and I think that is awfully important. A crucifix says far more than a lot of words from a preacher. And that really lies at the heart of the sacraments: the idea that you say things to each other and to God not with words but with very ordinary actions like eating, drinking, shaking hands.

Father Basil adds:

I've always been very struck by the way Jesus healed people by touching them. That touch was life-giving. And that way of looking at the human gesture, communicating the spiritual value, is what lies at the heart of the sacramental system.

David Isitt, an Anglican, gave me the clue that there is a distinction between priests who see themselves as prophets and those who see themselves as pastors.

And if you're a pastor and a listener, it leaves you drained of anything to say in a public way about race or nuclear disarmament.

I think that in the churches of the Reformation there is an enormous emphasis on 'the Word' and therefore words. But anyone in the full-time active pastoral ministry knows that in a great many instances it is not a matter of having something to say, but of some kind of contact. It may be a matter of touch – I was going to say, of smell and taste as well, but one can become a bit fanciful. But if you're a pastor you're not giving answers all the time. You're trying to help people to see, in what the old hymn calls 'the common things of life', a way into the eternal – which, I suppose, is what the sacramental principle is.

David Watson, the evangelical, agrees that

The whole of life is much more sacramental than some of us from a non-sacramental background tend to admit. Many of us require these personal touches without which we will become increasingly alienated from one another, or even from ourselves. We need that reassurance of each other's love and acceptance. And we need reassurance of God's love and acceptance in Christ. Sacrament is a very important thing.

Increasingly I find Christians of all denominations agreeing upon that. I have attended few communions more impressive or rapt in contemplation than at the High Kirk of the Church of Scotland in Edinburgh. But what does it mean? What is happening? In what sense can that bread and wine *be* the body and blood of Jesus?

The doctrine of transubstantiation – that the substance of the bread and wine are changed into the substance of Christ's body and blood at the moment of consecration – has caused endless argument and disunity among the churches. It goes back to the gospel statement of Jesus: 'This is My body . . . This is My blood . . .', and what the Church has done is to take Jesus' word for it, without pretending to know *how* it is done. Consecration, in the Roman view, effects a change in the inner reality of the bread and wine. The elements are not mere signs or symbols. Christ's body and blood become really present and are really eaten and drunk. But in fact, the original thirteenth-century doctrine of transubstantiation was far more spiritual than most shocked Protestants understand.

The 'substance' of which St Thomas Aquinas wrote was not material but metaphysical substance; he insisted that the physical or 'accidental' substance of the bread did not change at all, and he saw the doctrine as combating superstitious tales of the host dripping blood. But, with its subtlety, this it failed to do. Two centuries later, popular Catholicism had degenerated into just the sort of magical pseudo-sacramentalism that the reformers deplored. We find the Thirty-nine Articles insisting:

Transubstantiation in the Supper of the Lord cannot be proved by Holy Writ; but is repugnant to the plain words of Scripture . . . The Body of Christ is given, taken, and eaten, in the Supper, only after an heavenly and spiritual manner. And the mean whereby the Body of Christ is received and eaten in the Supper is Faith.

John Stott reflects that approach when he says:

It depends on the mood in which I receive it, and that is a very strong part of evangelical belief. One of the Thirty-nine Articles quotes St Augustine as saying that you can press with your teeth the sacrament of Christ's body without receiving Christ at all. It's not automatic. The sacraments are only efficacious if they are received worthily, with penitence and faith. So I believe that I receive Christ, not because He is in the bread and wine but because He is in the heart of those who receive the bread and wine believingly. Richard Hooker, the great Elizabethan, said, 'The presence of Christ is not in the sacrament but in the worthy recipient of the Sacrament.'

The basic significance of this – that the sacrament is not magic, but must be responded to in the right spirit to become effective – seems to me perfectly Catholic. St Augustine also says, 'A good man receives the sacrament and the reality of the sacrament; but a bad man receives only the sacrament and not the reality.' Putting it another way, fruitful reception depends upon disposition. What you get out of it depends upon what you believe about it – which is common sense. The Roman Church naturally expects its members to believe what it teaches: this is always much subtler than and sometimes quite different to what many non-Catholics suppose. For example, when it says Christ's body and blood become *really* present, it does not mean there is human flesh-protein and corpuscular fluid in the mouth. It means that the elements are endowed with a new meaning, a new reality as the body and blood of Christ. That is what they mean, so that is what they 'really' are. On a lower level, you might say that a piece of cloth and some coloured dyes, combined as the Union Jack, are endowed with a new reality as the national flag: though that reality only becomes fruitful if you are disposed to believe in what it stands for, if you have patriotism.

The fact that the Eucharist can have so many different meanings and so much depth, so much richness, is what places it with the Crucifixion at the heart of the Christian faith. If it had only one plain significance it would not satisfy so many in so many different ways. All over Britain, there are worship groups and house churches meeting together to share bread and wine without the help of clergy in ways that would horrify a strict church disciplinarian: officially they are not Eucharists at all, for the elements have not been consecrated by a priest; they are *agapae*, love-feasts, or re-enactments of the meal at Emmaus. But many of those who take part in them see them as much more. Una Kroll says she rarely meets God now in the institutional churches, but finds her relationship with Him 'in small groups of people in home Eucharists'.

For Dr Kroll, the real Church is a non-institutional one, 'The mystical Body of Christ, the company of people who serve Christ'; and that raises the delicate question of whether those who preside at her Eucharists are ordained priests with authority to consecrate. It seems that sometimes they are and sometimes they aren't:

The non-institutional Church throws up its own priests. Sometimes they coincide with what the Church of England has already authenticated as a priest. Sometimes they are not people whom any institution has dubbed priestly, but they are for me priestly people. If you take a sacrament as a visible and outward sign of an inward and spiritual grace, they make visible and enable me to partake of the inward and spiritual grace.

The heavy theology of the Eucharist sits quite lightly these days on many who take it very seriously. Neville Black thinks it all wrong to confine the Eucharist to church, anyway.

When Jesus sat round the table, broke bread and drank wine, that was the place for any group of people meeting. The church should be all over the place: when you meet with your family, when you meet your buddies in the pub, there ought to be an element of sacrament there. Yes, the sacrament is on offer in the church service, but that isn't the only place it's on offer.

Alison Adcock, Oxfordshire vicar's wife, could not believe the apostles had seen in their ceremony the idea of sacrifice:

I don't find any help in the 'sacrifice of the mass' idea. But I do find a great deal in the idea that we are sharing a fellowship meal in honour of Christ, and that somehow or other the spirit of Christ is among us at that time. I think meals are very holy things anyway. The first loving relationship we know is sharing food with someone else. I suppose that is something that a woman feels more strongly about than a man.

The sacrifice element in the mass takes us back to the difficulties we encountered in understanding the Crucifixion. Recent talks between Anglican and Roman Catholic theologians have tried to overcome some of these by developing the idea of the Holy Communion as *memorial*. Father Timothy Wright approved of this:

Whereas, at the Reformation, the Roman Catholic Church insisted on the repetition of the sacrifice – giving the impression that once and for all wasn't enough – the reformers wanted to exclude all mention of sacrifice, on the grounds that the one sacrifice was complete in itself and did not need repeating. Now the Jewish idea of memorial is not simply a recalling, it is a reliving: if you gave thanks for something, you always said what you gave thanks for. In the Eucharist, we hold that in the prayer of thanksgiving we are saying 'thank you' for the death of Christ, for the offering of His life to the Father for us. And as we say thank you, so we re-enact, we relive that experience. We are not repeating it; because it only happened once and *can* only happen once. But we are really reliving it with this congregation at this moment.

Well: ingenious. Sometimes I get the impression that the theologians are making their progress towards unity by so blurring the meaning of words that they merge into a continuous cloud. If you are the sort of person who is bothered by the fear that Christ is belittled by the symbolic repetition of His sacrifice, I doubt if you will be won over by calling it a 'reliving memorial'. But I suspect that growing numbers of Christians are impatient with verbal analyses of what would never have become the central *action* of the faith if words could have sufficed. There must surely be *some* words, or we would have no idea at all of what we were reaching towards. Indeed, there are enough to reach in several directions, as our witnesses have shown. But even if you cannot accept the idea of a sacrifice at all, you can still come to terms with communion and may be happy enough to share the Lord's Table with people who find at it different meanings from your own.

The two ancient families of Christendom, the Latins and the Orthodox, remain insistent that we cannot share with them unless we accept their meanings. Basil Hume says: 'I believe that this is truly the body and blood of Jesus Christ, and if my neighbour does not believe this, then we are not one in our faith.' Metropolitan Anthony tells me:

I do believe that when we address to the Lord our prayer to send down His Holy Spirit upon this bread and wine, it does happen. I have no theory about how it happens. But it happens with the same simple certainty which I would attach to the incarnation. If God could unite Himself to a human flesh and soul, he can unite Himself as completely to this bread and wine. And when we receive communion, I believe that God reaches out to us on the most primitive and simple level. A babe can receive a small particle of bread and a drop of wine, and with it be reached by God.

This is extremely direct. There is no question of the babe's 'disposition' making any difference. Alas, neither Metropolitan Anthony nor Cardinal Hume may offer their God to me in a particle of bread, for I am not of their churches. It seems a pity, for they are men I revere and we have so much else of the faith in common. Archbishop Runcie and many of the others would, I fancy, be more accommodating. But would I, in fact, approach them for it? As a sign of fellowship with my brothers and sisters, I well might – indeed, I have done. The question is, do I believe myself to be accepting the body and blood of Christ?

Now that I understand a great deal more about the sacraments than I did a year ago, I would certainly not regard the elements as mere bread and wine – any more than I regard the Crucifixion as a mere execution. I can see sacramentalism as a kind of action-poetry, another language. It is also a discipline, both in the sense of instruction and of salutary duty. I think I would come close to accepting the idea of *transignification*, offered by the Dutch theologian Schillebeeckx and others: that the bread takes on a new *significance* as the body of Christ, so that in that sense you could say its reality was changed.

At any rate it is clear to me that it is immature to regard the sacraments as being a form of priestly magic. They are something God does, not what we do – and to which we respond. But I still have one last reservation, which some will call an excuse: if the bread and wine really are what they are said to be, then to take them in that sense I am not worthy.

CHAPTER TWELVE
Some Hope!

'And now abideth faith, hope, charity, these three; but the greatest of these is charity', says St Paul.

The most neglected of these is hope, though. The whole of this book has been about faith, which is the Christian's response in charity to charity – in love to love. But hope is the neglected member of another trinity, a wishy-washy virtue which has never much appealed to the classical thinkers of the Church, a kind of second-rate, watered-down faith. I *hope* for life eternal suggests that my *faith* in it is less than total.

But just as the suffering and vulnerability of God has given new life and meaning to the Christian gospel, so the virtue of hope has assumed a new significance during the last twenty years. In the past it had been seen as a kind of supercharged confidence in God's goodwill, made possible by grace and betrayed by despair. Since the German Protestant theologian Moltmann published his *Theology of Hope* in 1967, hope has been taken up as an imperative, a command to man, to take responsibility for the Kingdom of God on earth; something which (it is argued) is quite clearly required in the gospels. The theology of hope does not just look upwards to the life eternal, the life after death (though that is part of it); it looks forward into the earthly future and is therefore partly political. Ortho*doxy* (right doctrine) is not enough. Ortho*praxis* (right action) matters too. And away we go into Latin American liberation theology, where the mighty are to be put down from their seat and the hungry and meek are to be exalted. But even this is not its own justification, for hope requires that everything – including the Church itself – be judged and perfected according to the hope of the Kingdom.

Hope, of course, puts down pessimism, and the greatest of all Christian hopes – demonstrated by Christ Himself – is the hope of resurrection after death. But you cannot have one without the other. The Resurrection affirms death as strongly as it does life. Everything we do happens in the context of our approaching end: only God gives us hope of anything more, and that makes the Christian appear deluded both to the pessimist who sees no meaning at all in life and to the humanistical optimist who sees no transcendent need for one. What hope does for the believing Christian is to take him out of his pious, contemplative backwater and put him into a continuous flow that sweeps him purposefully through this life into the next. That flow is the flow of all humanity struggling to realise the Kingdom, and we can no longer justify our course in terms of our own solitary salvation. Time and again in the Bible, hope is a collective thing.

Hope, then, is Christian purpose in life and death. It concerns the ethics of our life on earth and our expectations of life after death. Inevitably there is greater fascination with the latter than the former, for while life on earth is an unquestionable fact and offers a wide choice of more or less workable standards, life after death is not demonstrable (my apologies to the Spiritualists here) and even the gospels have very little to tell us about it. A more obviously-minded God would have clinched everything by providing us with ready access to the after-life, including graphic first-hand descriptions of the torments suffered by the damned and the bliss enjoyed by the virtuous. Reasonably enough, in His own terms, He seems to have decided that a lower level of existence would make little sense of a higher one and has kept the door closed.

So what hope has the Christian, here on earth? Change and decay in all around we see. The hosts of Midian prowl and prowl around. All is sin and shame. Or is it? 'I don't think there is anything to be gloomy about,' says Michael Green, 'Jesus is alive and doing things!'

'We celebrate that God is still on the throne, the Lord who reigns, and whether it will be through suffering or not, we know that for Christians the best is yet to be,' agrees David Watson. 'That is what we have to hold on to. Hope, I think, is a forgotten theological virtue.' He goes on:

If you want to see New Testament Christianity today, you've got to go to the Third World, where they've lost everything that's worth having materially – or have never had it. But they have that vibrant faith which bursts through suffering and pain, oppression and disaster. I don't think it's just escapism, because they have to face the realities of it all, but they do celebrate that God is amongst them, that God loves them and God cares for them.

Could we recreate anything like that in Britain?

I think so, though you may have to wait until the hard shell of apathy is further cracked and broken. It may be only when things become more serious than they are now in terms of bitterness, violence and even revolution that people may again cry out to God. It's hardly a compliment to God if we turn to him because there's nothing else to be had. But He, in His divine humility, is willing to accept us even on those terms. I am longing to see this nation so broken in its pride, arrogance, apathy and cynicism that eventually we do cry out to God, who saves us and is alive today.

Our hope, from this view, lies in surrender to faith, lies in the celebrated Protestant doctrine of justification by faith. The Baptist Howard Williams says:

The emphasis there is upon the fact that you're accepted by God before you do anything at all about it. It doesn't depend upon your achievement or any merit you may have. It doesn't depend upon you being a good boy. It depends rather simply upon the nature of God Himself and the way he is related to people. Justification by faith means that a person is set right with God by the very act of God Himself.

So our hope, our forgiveness, justification and purpose are there all the time in God, if only we will recognise that and reach out for them.

But if Christianity does offer hope, there are still many people who worry desperately about whether the way of Christ, the way of love and self-giving, actually works in our world. Peter Cornwell thinks:

It matters greatly whether one believes Jesus to be a sudden irruption of loving and caring who was ultimately ground down by the forces of violence and injustice, or whether this love is rooted in the reality of God Himself. The world is full of wilting idealists. We're at a moment when the optimism drains away and people wonder whether this love business works. They collapse into cynicism and nihilism. But we need to put hope into our love – that hope which arises from seeing in Jesus the ultimate reality of God Himself.

Britain is a bad place for seeing such hope, but I, too, have seen it in the Third World. Eric James says:

In a modern state like India the state is saying to the Church, 'Don't talk of love – show me!' You are not allowed just to be a missionary. I've seen a lot of Vellore Hospital, southwest of Madras, which I suppose is as good a piece of Christian work as there is in the world. It affects the whole Indian medical system, showing them how to retain doctors in a country which is being seduced all the time by oil people in the Gulf who can pay British and American salaries for doctors. At Vellore they've learnt how get Indian doctors to relate to a community of commitment which keeps them where they are, and sends them into the villages when most doctors in the secular system want to go into the cities.

More aggressively, there is the liberation theology of Latin America, much criticised by Doctor Edward Norman in his Reith Lectures. Dr Norman believes this theology is not really, as it claims to be, the authentic voice of the oppressed, but a humanistic, secular idealism imposed on the Third World by a westernised elite in the churches. 'In their death agonies', he says, 'the Western churches are distributing the causes of their own sickness – the politicisation of religion – to their healthy offspring in the developing world.' To Dr Norman, our liberal internationalist churchmen are deceiving themselves in imagining that they are taking Christian values into politics; what has happened is precisely the reverse. They are not pursuing hope, but absorption in the pagan secular world.

Professor Maurice Wiles, acknowledging he speaks from a rather comfortable position, thinks the liberationists have made the mistake of identifying their views with the entire gospel: 'But that is their reaction against a theology which has not addressed itself sufficiently to the problems of political oppression and tyranny.'

James Whyte accepts that there is an element of truth in what Norman says:

I read a book the other day by some younger theologians and thought it was the student revolution of 1968 in long trousers. The same kind of utter certainties, self-righteousness, no possible debate with anyone who doesn't agree with them. But on the other hand, Norman has a coldness and indifference to the suffering of the world which is absolutely frightening in a man who calls himself a Christian. His book is astonishingly cynical. I found both him and the people he criticises misinterpreting Christianity quite radically. Those people regard the Church not in terms of its faith and gospel but in terms of left-wing political action. But Norman equally has no gospel. His understanding of religion is not good news but a kind of spiritual cultivation, whereby you are going to be saved if you cultivate your soul properly. But Christianity is the good use of the love of God, which issues forth in the love of neighbour, and in the name of God against injustice and cruelty.

Enough, perhaps, of that particular theological odium, for it has had plenty of time on the air already. There are workers for justice and peace, like Anne Forbes, a Roman Catholic, who see the life of action and the life of prayer as inseparable:

I must be able to reflect and to pray with the people I'm working with. The sort of work we are doing is draining, often dispiriting. We have to keep reminding ourselves about the Christian hope. And it is only by praying together and celebrating the Eucharist that we get the courage to go on and to discern the direction in which we are supposed to be going.

Anne Forbes went out to the Philippines a few years ago, where the situation is rather like that in Latin America:

I came back feeling that we Christians in the West were fat, flabby and unhealthy; and that out there they were fit and lean. They spend a lot more time reading the gospel than we do; and both by their understanding of it and by their struggle to serve the poor,

191

they are much healthier Christians. Their integration, almost their sanity, is a source of inspiration to people like me.

So does the Christian hope demand that we all take vows of poverty? Peter Baelz thinks not necessarily:

I don't think Jesus was in favour of poverty as such, though He felt the poor were more open to the realities of life than those who had blinded themselves with possessions. It may well be that if you think the Kingdom is coming, you should put other things on one side. But if the world goes on, as it has, then I think human flourishing is as much part of the Christian as it was of the Jewish gospel. Poverty, like suffering, is not good in itself. It may be turned to good. Certainly I think it needs to be fought against.

Archbishop Worlock, contemplating the gospel for the unemployed, emphasises that it includes honesty and responsibility. 'It isn't just a question of protection for the working man. It also sets standards for him in terms of moral living and concern for other people. There are an awful lot of tricks of the trade.' The Archbishop found himself recalling, from his days in Stepney, that every time a docker had his foot crushed by falling cargo, another man would shout out: 'I done that!' Insurance did not cover a man if it was his own fault. 'In so far as it was a pretty dishonest insurance system,' said the Archbishop, 'one used to talk to them a great deal about concern for one's neighbour and leave the Lord to work out the rest.'

So realising the Christian hope can get one tangled up in Christian ethics, and that applies to the Christian employer as much as to the Christian working man. Derek Worlock had lost the battle to keep open a Liverpool sugar refinery which had been noted for its high output and superb industrial relations:

In the end, the men were saying bitterly, 'Industrial relations have nothing to do with the closure. It's just a matter of where they can make the most money.' Now, you can understand the employer saying, 'We have to be viable.' But I think one also has to say, 'Think very hard before you abandon the people who have been responsible with you for what prosperity you have.'

192

Once again, it is pure folk religion to imagine that Christianity 'makes you good', that it has all the answers at the back of the book, or that there are no answers to be found anywhere else. It has always incorporated large slabs of what is known as 'natural law' – that kindness is good, cruelty bad, co-operation to be admired, selfishness abhorred. Most of the moral standards of Christendom are to be found in other civilisations and can easily be justified by a humanist. But James Whyte says:

There are two specifically Christian things which I don't think you really find anywhere else. One is the emphasis on love as the supreme moral standard – together with the understanding of love that comes through the self-giving of Jesus on the Cross. And the second, linked with it, is the doctrine of forgiveness – the kind of love which repairs and heals relationships that are broken.

This, I venture to suggest, is the least employed of Christian virtues in public life. Could we – would we dare to – *forgive* the IRA for its murders, the Russians for invading Afghanistan, the street gangs for burning down Moss Side?

One obstacle to hope is that we find it hard enough to forgive ourselves: we handicap ourselves with the weight of our own failure. Yet here is another of Christianity's unique contributions, that being founded upon an apparent failure (the humiliating execution of its leader) it meets and tackles failure head on. Says James Whyte:

In that sense it stands opposed to all the natural standards of the world. Christians have been very slow and reluctant to think that through in relation to their understanding of God: to see God as vulnerable Himself; not, as it were, to separate the suffering of Christ from the impassibility of the Father, but to see that God Himself is vulnerable and accepts failure.

The Christian hope, then, is not the hope of inevitable success in our own short-range terms; but the sure hope that whatever we suffer, the indestructible God suffers with us. It is a strenuous hope, not a triumphal one.

Throughout the interviews which helped me on my progress I was aware of one particular group of pilgrims to whom strenuousness came naturally: the women. Statistically, I may not have met enough of them. Rightly or wrongly – and I think wrongly – our churches are still led and dominated by men; men are the articulators and spokesmen of our culture as it now is. They are the ones with the pastoral experience, they have established the language of theology. But I sense, welling up around them, hitherto submerged strata of feminine spirituality. Spirituality is not a word I very much care to use, but I mean by it here an intuitive knowledge of the divine, drawn more from experience than from reading and manipulating words, and expressed in equally practical terms.

Feminism, as such, is not necessarily part of it. I have met spiritually powerful women who have no interest whatever in becoming priests and are even quite content with the Catholic men-only clergy. I have met men, too – and ordained ones – who insist that until women are accepted by the Church as equals, and the feminine is fully integrated into the Church, men themselves will always be distorted. Peter Bide, of Christ Church, is an admirer of the fourteenth-century mystic, Juliana of Norwich who

long ago learnt to call God Mother, and found no problem about doing so. I don't see why we should be having all this fuss about it now. This woman seems to me to have a closer grasp of what our contemporaries understand about the nature of God and Jesus than any other individual I can think of. But it's not a man's vision at all – it's a woman's – and I owe an enormous amount to it. Why we don't make use of that kind of contribution, which lies bubbling away in our churches, I don't know. Or rather, I do. A large number of men live in a society which doesn't exist any more.

What does still exist, so far as the Church of England, the Roman Catholic and the Orthodox churches are concerned, is a ban on the ordination of women as priests. Nevertheless, the Archbishop of Canterbury acknowledges that 'women have wits as well as wombs and we ought to recognise that fact'. Alison Adcock, a licensed reader in the Archbishop's communion, does not entirely hold with the notion of a distinct feminine spirituality, because most people have got tough and tender aspects, which we call male and feminine – which causes more trouble really to men, because they feel ashamed of being tender. That's a terrible thing and probably responsible for a lot of the misery of the world.

Eleanor Barnes points out that many of the great monastic leaders had

a good and wholesome link with the opposite sex. One of the sad things about modern life is that the minute you mention sex, people limit it to bedtime, and it isn't . . . I think women are better at understanding sexuality as being part of the way one expresses one's whole being. And I think women are more practical. Their attitude is usually geared to the realities of life and death, the messy things that happen; and yet, through those messy things, an understanding of the beauty and grandeur of it all. It is less easy for men to be involved in birth, and their traditions are much less concerned with death, too. It is interesting that the medical profession, which is predominantly male, is terrified of death and sees it as a failure; whereas women more readily understand that death can be an achievement. Women were there at Christ's death and resurrection. They had this fearlessness of the body, this willingness to sink all and follow, even if it didn't make sense. Whereas the apostles were jolly doubtful. It's all very well to blame St Thomas; but in fact the others all stood round putting their fingers in the wounds before they really cottoned on – doubting lot!

Valerie Fisher is not sure women can actually be spared for the priesthood:

There are so many other things for us to do. I feel it is going to lead to something far more important than laying hands on women and even sticking their bottoms on diocesan benches. We don't want that, in particular. I think it could be that a different attitude to ministry will emerge.

Rosemary Haughton, deep in the Christian communities movement, seems to have found a ministry of her own. She sees her groups as evidence of the feminine element breaking through. 'Over the last couple of generations it has been coming to the surface very strongly, and because of that it has also produced a violent reaction. In the Catholic Church the fear of the feminine has been tremendous.'

Catholic women are often told that their position in the Church is secured by the figure of Our Lady. Mrs Haughton recalled that when Pius XII defined the dogma of the bodily Assumption of the Virgin into Heaven, in 1950, the psychiatrist Jung had described it as the most important event for four hundred years.

He was saying this was a symbol of something happening in the whole culture; saying the feminine was not something we have to push underground, but at the heart of human experience at its most divine.

We know so little about Mary as a human being, though. I think she was a very powerful woman and perhaps very difficult for the early church to deal with. I wonder whether her disappearance from the scene isn't because, in fact, they didn't know what to do with her. Jung suggested we might devise a Quaternity to take the place of the Trinity, and it seems to me that does express the fact that the feminine is part of the whole – that we can't separate it out.

Margaret Bowker does want to see women ordained; but

I do not want them to lose what they have had since the time of Jesus – this warmth, this prayer-centredness. You will find, for instance, in the Anglican communion, more contemplative nuns than monks; and among the laity, many more women giving time to listening prayer. If the ordination of women meant they gave that up and put on dog-collars, it would be a disaster. But prayer doesn't just come to women wrapped up in a parcel, with love from God. It takes time and hard work. One postmistress once told me that as she cycled around with the post, she prayed as she went. I wondered how many male postmen were doing the same.

Mother Mary Clare, who presides over a religious house in Oxford, thinks:

There is something in the female, in her need of love and to give love, which comes out in the silent, compassionate awareness of prayer. But if only our brothers had more opportunity to be still, to be quiet, you might find the contemplative nature of our male counterparts would very much expand.

We have drifted away somewhat from Christian hope in action. But several of the women I talked to showed that, too, more vividly than the men. Mary Cullen, a Scots Catholic, stays at home with her three small children

and life is very mundane. Yet as a Christian I do believe that life is transformed by Christ and baptism, and therefore love doesn't become a great big squashy thing: it becomes a matter of responding all the time. I don't think anything dramatic is usually asked of people; they're usually asked to respond in small ways, but it's a total of small responses that changes people, and that's what I mean by love.

Christian hope shone through the lives of two women Salvationists I met. Christine Johnson, who works in the appalling surroundings of an alcoholics' clinic accepts, very simply, that the same power that raised Jesus from the dead

is available in us. Since I came to this appointment I have questioned my faith and grown in it more than I ever did before. Putting it to the test proves it, more and more; and seeing that there is power available to each of us.

Her fellow Salvationist, Christine Parkin, has something more like a parish beat. 'If I am open to the tramp who comes to the door for the fourth time that week for his cup of coffee, or spare the time to listen to the deep needs of people . . .' But often she must be let down and betrayed by people?

Oh, I coped with that one long ago. It doesn't worry me. I feel that my responsibility is to the Lord, and so is theirs. It's the Lord who is betrayed. People have to stand on their own two feet and look the Lord in the face for themselves.

It is the classic Christian hope that this is precisely what we shall do when we die. Yet not all, even among the women, were so sure of that. When I asked Mrs Adcock what she expected after death, she answered bleakly:

I'm terrified there'll be more life. I don't want to have any more experience after death. I think of that picture by Munch called 'The Scream' – the scream that goes on and on and on. Life would be totally meaningless if it went on for ever.

But what does Metropolitan Anthony expect after death? Firmly, 'Life. I have a small notion of life from living in the body, and I feel a moment must come when life must burst, or dance, in triumph; and that is what I expect from eternal life.'

'I expect to be dead,' said Father Butterworth, rather obviously.

At least, that's as far as I can go in any literal or descriptive form. On the other hand, the hope that I have assures me that in some way which must be indescribable, since I don't have the concepts of the other world in which I might describe it, I will achieve communion with God, which will finally make me the person I was always meant to be.

Dame Cecily Saunders, pioneer of the hospice movement for the incurable, has helped thousands to set out on their last journey. She believes death is the ending of one kind of life and the beginning of another 'in which there is continuity'. What makes her so confident of this?

Because we spend all our lifetime learning to love – and the most important thing about us is our capacity to relate to other people – it just doesn't fit in with the rest of nature for there to be a total end of something like that. That could be wishful thinking, but I feel, like Pascal, that if I betted on that I would not be the loser.

And what about Heaven and Hell? Says Dame Cecily,

Heaven, certainly has meaning for me. We shall be satisfied. I don't think it's going to be sitting with our hands folded. I happen to love singing in a choir, so some of the pictures given us of Heaven do in fact mean something to me. As for Hell, I can imagine turning away into my own darkness, but I hate to think of anyone else doing it. However, I certainly don't think that I'm fit as I am now to step into eternity. I hope that something will happen to make me more fit to do so, and I suppose that is what is meant by Purgatory. It seems to me most helpful. Judgment, you know, means setting things right; it just doesn't mean punishment.

Mother Mary Clare, too, thinks of life after death in terms of the Bach Choir singing Elgar's *Dream of Gerontius*. 'Take me away, take me away . . .' sings the tenor soloist. And Lord Ramsey fully expects to be taken away to some sort of Purgatory:

I expect it will be painful, but I know I need a great deal of cleaning up. I do not suppose that just because I die, I'm going to get the beatific vision at once. I'm certainly sure that I'm not. But this deeper relationship with God, which I believe is meant to lead on to the actual vision of God, can't be just a private affair; because to be with God is inevitably social and community. And that causes me to have the expectation of seeing and knowing all sorts of people I've seen and known in the past, and perhaps a great deal more as well. How it is going to be possible to manage all this I simply don't know.

It's always a pity to leave out Hell, because we do need to warn ourselves of it. I believe in Hell in this sense: that our free will is a condition of our being moral people, and if our free will were to go on preferring selfish isolation to being joined with the love of God, our free will is quite capable of doing that – and that is Hell. I believe Hell to be the stewing in our own juice, rather than sharing in the love of God, because we are silly enough to go on wanting it to be so. I think we ought to warn ourselves about it, rather than lecture other people.

Perhaps all the Christian should really require of his hope is Mother Juliana's assurance that, 'All shall be well, and all shall be well, and all manner of thing shall be well.' But the fact is, that very free will of ours keeps us trying to peep beyond the veil. If there is anything there at all, it stands to reason that nothing we can imagine with earthly senses – be it choirs or clouds or meadows – can correspond with what we shall one day experience. Bishop John V. Taylor gave me a kind of metaphysical picture which I think will always be my preferred one:

What do I expect? Something much bigger than I can imagine, and this frightens me. At the moment when time comes to an end for me, I expect to be confronted with the whole of reality in one impact, streaming towards me. At that moment, I am either suddenly going to find it in myself to spread my arms, say yes, and jump into the stream; or else I am going to shrink back and say no. I think all the little decisions I am making here in this short life are the decisions as to whether I will ultimately say yes to reality, or whether I will shut myself up in fear and say no – either preparing me for that big yes, or turning me into the kind of person who will finally shrink into nothing.

No chance there of Purgatory. Purgatory, it seems, is now.

There are a fortunate few which knows they are saved already. Salvationists speak of their dead as 'Promoted to Glory'. Bishop Reindorp, who could certainly have my testimonial if it would do him any good, regards the afterlife as

A most thrilling prospect: a liberation. I've got a child in Paradise, and all sorts of people will be there: many whom we have forgotten about, and many people whom the world didn't think much about. It won't be a static condition, all stained glass windows: we shall be given work to do.

'I don't think it's going to be the sort of place where it's going to be quiet,' says Neville Black.

I hope there are going to be football games and a Cup Tie in Heaven. Sorry if that sounds flippant, but I don't want it just to be all angels and wings. It's going to be full of life for me. Me with others, and all of us in some wonderful way together.

But prove it, prove it – and of course you cannot prove it, or it would be another dreary biological fact instead of a Christian hope. I have thought myself close to death, rigged up with wires and tubes in the intensive care unit, twice in my life; and I have to say that I was much less worried about life after death than I am about the doctrine of the Trinity. Whatever it is, I find myself quite confident that it is all being taken care of. I shall leave the last word to Father Timothy Firth:

Years ago, it suddenly hit me that either the whole thing is absurd or it isn't. And the way that all human beings live gives it away that actually we do not base our lives on the absurd. We're thinking of our welfare, other people's welfare, making plans, shying away from suffering and pain. The evidence is there, we give ourselves away, that we do not believe life is absurd. Certainly some of the finest people I know are open and professed atheists. They say that when they die, that's it – finish. And yet the very way that they live, as an example to me as a Christian, gives them away. But when I say that to them, they get absolutely mad with me and say, 'You're cheating because you've dragged in faith again!' And I am cheating, in a way, yes.

For cheating, read hoping. What else can a Christian do?

CHAPTER THIRTEEN
Mr Ready-to-Halt's Crutches

But *am* I a Christian? Or have I in this pilgrimage at least made some progress towards becoming one? Cardinal Hume allowed me to keep my conscience and was kind enough to imply that I *was* a Christian, if not a very mature one; and I am inclined to accept his judgment. Archbishop Runcie thought there were some essentials of the faith that I really ought to hold – like the resurrection and divinity of Jesus – but granted me a wide variety of expression. Others were more demanding.

Bishop Taylor of St Albans thought the irreducible minimum of the Christian faith was:

actually accepting Jesus Christ as the Son of God. There's no question of just admiring Him as a prophet or fitting Him into some pantheon of other gods. There is a sense in which he is *the* Son of God. I would never question another person's profession of faith. I may say to myself, 'That person has a great deal further to go along the way before I find myself in cahoots with him – but he has an incipient, unformed or developing faith,' and faith is always a crescendo of commitment and understanding. I am not in the business of assessing other people's acceptability to God – He is the judge. I'm in the business of saying to people that if they want to be regarded as Christians they must come to Christ as the Son of God and give their lives in obedience to Him.

But although I do now have a meaning for 'the Son of God' and could even say 'Jesus was God', I have my doubts whether I and the bishop would mean the same by those words, let alone by 'obedience to Him'.

I am greatly stirred when John Stott tells me:

Christianity is not primarily a theological system, an ethical system, a ritual system, a social system or an ecclesiastical system – it is a person: it's Jesus Christ, and to be a Christian is to know Him and to follow Him and believe in Him.

But on the one hand, do I know and follow the same Jesus as Stott? On the other, it is very difficult to detach oneself from all those secondary systems, or pretend they are not there. For better or worse, Christ does not stand unaided. There *is* Christian theology, Christian liturgy, the Church, and I am now more than ever convinced that there must be. They would be nothing without the figure of Jesus, but given Him and given the nature of humanity, they are bound to follow.

I am aware that I lack the experience some Christians call 'being born again', or at least I lack anything in the style of a Damascus Road experience. My enlightenment came more clinically on the psychiatrist's couch, though I value it no less. When I asked Michael Green if it was compulsory for me to be 'knocked all of a heap by the Holy Spirit' in order to be a Christian, I was relieved to hear him say:

Certainly not. This is a stupid misunderstanding which some enthusiastic Christians have caused and which can be rather revolting and man-centred. The important thing is that He has decided for us, not us for Him, and that is what the cross means. And the resurrection means that He says: 'Gerald, Michael, I accept you.' All the time we respond that we're going to run our own show, we don't get the encouragement and relationship we are meant to have. But as His warmth thaws us and we throw off the clothes that have been getting in the way, it begins to *happen*: very much like falling in love.

Well, am I in love with Christ? Here again, I squirm and start taking refuge behind the meaning of words. It is no good pretending I am not a bit of a sexist, and that love for me does not imply an element of possession. If I make a special effort, I accept that it ought to mean complete equality. But I cannot own Christ selfishly, and I certainly cannot claim equality with Him: any pretence I make at these is true only in a limited, poetic sense. Harry Williams tells me 'God is my deepest self, He is what I am'; but he also tells me 'God is infinitely other and greater than I', and I agree with both.

There stands another problem: that while Christ may be

so like God that as far as we are concerned He *is* God – we have met nothing closer – yet we can dimly sense unexplored acres of God which make Him even greater than the Jesus we know. The Church and its scriptures offer me, through their mediation, a knowable Christ; but can I honestly say that the divine I know is Jesus and nothing else? If it were, why should we have the Trinity, the three ways of being God? In spite of my journalistic instinct for getting back to the original – an ambition I can never fulfil, and which would probably disappoint me if I could – I do in fact welcome the depth and richness of the structure which has been built upon it. We cannot be first-century Christians, for we are not first-century people. I value Ivor Smith Cameron's remark: 'My highest vocation is not to be a Christian. My highest vocation is to be a human being; that's what God has created me as, and my Christian equipment is to offer me all the resources for being human.'

The Baptist Michael Taylor weaves me in and out of that stream of thought, saying:

For me, Christianity is about the Kingdom, not about the Church: it has to do with human growth and development, not church growth and development. I find it almost ridiculous that some people can get so excited about converting half a dozen more people, instead of altering the quality of life that everyone shares so unequally.

I don't think Christianity can be defined in terms of acceptable teachings, ethics, liturgies, bishops or anything else. I don't think there are Christian 'right answers' which you have to hold. For me, being a Christian is going back to the very simple, primitive confession that Jesus is Lord – which had overtones for the early Christians it doesn't have for me. But I think it is saying that in my experience that person, who lived and died two thousand years ago, is the most illuminating spot in history as to what goodness, truth, beauty, God, human life are all about. To be a Christian is to be overwhelmingly impressed by that, and to try to live one's life being true to it. After that, I think there is very little required common ground between Christians: immediately, everybody starts going along different paths. That is inevitable. I do not think heresy is coming to the wrong conclusions. It is coming to any conclusion alone; no longer listening to all the other voices in history and the world around you, but coming to your own conclusions without being enriched by others, being jolted by others, and being called on to something where all of you are converted into something better than any of them.

I hope that, in these pages, I have at least listened, and that my heresies are now less solitary than they used to be.

My favourite character in that great *Progress* from which I have stolen my title is Bunyan's Mr Ready-to-Halt; one with whom I feel a considerable affinity, for he travelled on crutches and kept company with Mr Feeble-Mind ('a very ignorant Christian' who 'if I hear any rejoice in the Lord, it troubles me because I cannot do so too'.) I take it that Mr Ready-to-Halt's name means that he is prone to stumble, rather than that he is on the point of abandoning his journey; for he goes on quite gamely and even offers Mr Feeble-Mind the loan of one of his crutches. The point is that Mr Ready-to-Halt needs propping up 'on the one hand and on the other' and dares not stand upon his own two legs. Dare I, having listened to so many good pilgrims, throw away my crutches and take my stand upon the way that leads to the Celestial City? Can I even see such a path?

I think I have to say once more that I see a number of paths, many of them converging and all leading in the same direction. Having started from so many different points, I cannot bring myself to say that one is right and all the others are wrong; nor do I find more than a handful of pilgrims claiming that.

Perhaps I should say a word here to my unbelieving, humanist and atheist friends, most of whom, I am sure, are as happy as I and far more useful and moral – which may be one reason why I need religion and they do not. It cannot be said too often that the Christian knows he is a sinner and that is why he seeks Christ (though I grant that the Church has often mishandled the concept of sin). I grant, too, that many non-believers have deep spiritual experience and satisfaction, often through the arts. I am not claiming that my experience and satisfaction are *better* than theirs (*better* is quite meaningless here), but they are different. The fact that unbelievers do not feel the need for them does not mean that I don't, that I am deluded, that they do not exist. Nor can it be argued that because it is possible to lead a good life without God, therefore God does not exist. God does not make us believe in Him: that would be a denial of free will, and God cannot be love, or we love Him, without freedom.

At once the unbeliever will protest that I am making self-fulfilling definitions. But so is the unbeliever. He or she is insisting that nothing that cannot be demonstrated by measurement and logic can be believed, and that we cannot speak of a true experience that cannot be demonstrated and repeated for others – though, in fact, some unbelievers *do* speak of inner, private experiences which they tend to describe in aesthetic rather than religious terms. I don't blame them for getting cross when believers insist these are apprehensions of the divine.

It seems to me that my experience does include awarenesses that are not measurable or demonstrable, and I have tried to indicate the quality of my belief in them by preferring the word 'trust'. Clearly I don't believe in God in the same way that I believe in the existence of a certain well-known political leader. But I think I have very powerful experiences of God, as a result of which I *trust* in Him very much more than I trust in the leader. If I were able to prove the existence of God in the same way that I can prove the existence of the leader, there would be no point in His being God, or in us being human as we understand those terms. But on the basis of my experience and trust, I find the Christian God hypothesis confirmed as the best way of making sense of my life – and in spite of myself, I have been drawn to the conviction that it does make sense. Not total sense, maybe, but I have a strong sense of sense.

Some of my Quaker friends may be critical of me for tolerating, in these pages, too dogmatic and human-like an image of God. They would probably prefer me to leave well alone things that we cannot possibly know. I began this journey disinclined to entertain the notion of doctrine, which it seemed to me was devised to shut some people in, others out, and to discourage new insights upon the truth. But I have become more tolerant of doctrine (without feeling obliged to subscribe to it myself) for three reasons.

First was the communication argument advanced by Professor Bowker: that it is necessary to limit and bind up a representation of a truth in order to protect it from dissolution and be able to pass it on at all. Second was the realisation that while all doctrine is incomplete, provisional, just a beginning, it is necessary to have something firm to work with. You cannot dig a hole with a rough sketch of a spade: you must have a well-forged blade firmly fixed to a handle.

My third reason for coming to terms with doctrine was a growing sense of solidarity with the communion of saints: by which I mean the general continuity of Christians, their communal subjectivity, up to the present day. Of course the way they think and the language they use varies over the centuries – Don Cupitt does not even believe that St Paul shared our concept of 'a fact' – but it seems to me that we are not totally alienated, that we can still grasp roughly what they are getting at, and that we must acknowledge, when we read the gospels or the Early Fathers or Luther or Newman, that these people did not have inferior minds to ours, that they were not deluded fools, that they are brothers and sisters on the same pilgrimage as ourselves. Not everything that was good enough for them will do for us, for we are living in a different century, a different culture; but it is stupid to throw away all their equipment and their textbooks.

Among these are those two great sources of authority, the Bible and the Church. To ask anyone 'Do you believe the Bible is true?' and demand the answer 'yes' or 'no' seems to me as unfair as to ask, 'Have you stopped beating your wife?' of somebody who has never started. True in what sense? Can any Christian mean to set the Bible up like the Koran as the word-for-word dictation of Jehovah? Must we believe that there really was a talking snake in the Garden of Eden, or that Moses saw the back parts of God, or that we are all forbidden to wear clothing of mixed fibres? Surely not;

though we need not doubt that the original writers believed in the holiness of what they wrote, that they meant what they said and that we, too, can extract meaning for ourselves if we use the disciplines of interpretation. None of the conservative evangelicals to whom I spoke denied the necessity of interpretation or for putting the Bible into the context of its times. Several of my witnesses agreed with the Jewish complaint that Christians have extracted quite illegitimate meanings from Hebrew texts. It seems to me that the Bible is a unique and extraordinary collection of books of several different types and of deep penetration into the natures of God and man. But to make it a clearly infallible guide to anything would be to rule out the possibility of free will, and therefore the God of love.

The same is true of the Church. If it were always right, if its doctrines were always obvious and complete, we should soon have found that we had no option but to become the slaves of perfection. We should have nothing to reach towards and no room for growth, besides committing the dangerous error of mistaking men for angels.

I think, myself, that the infallibility of church assemblies is as dubious as the infallibility of popes. Truth is not necessarily ascertained by majority vote, and not more than a fragment of the truth about God will ever be known by any means. The best we can do is to acknowledge as wide a Church as we possibly can (inevitably it will be suborganised into churches) and to maintain open dialogue within it, neither seeking to compel others to accept our convictions nor rejecting theirs as mad. Some will press forward down paths that lead nowhere; others will hang back and refuse to move at all; from time to time, as in the past, the whole body will get stuck in a confused mêlée; and at others it will assume a unity and discipline that will carry it forward in impressive style. But it has been on the road for almost two thousand years, and I think it is not for any individual of seventy years' span to usurp the role of the Holy Spirit by presuming to say where it should go.

There have been times on this pilgrimage when I have been tempted to lash out at the Church and its churches.

How absurd it is! How smug, how feeble, how cowardly, hypocritical, second-rate, class blind, irrelevant. I cannot help sympathising with Donald Reeves when he says:

The most robust Christianity I know is that coming out of Latin America, men and women regarded as subversive, in danger of their lives, but shining examples of all I call grace – full human beings whom God has in some way touched. They are in a terrible situation, and we blind ourselves to the fact that the situation here, too, is more terrible than we know. The Church of England simply fails to understand the contradictions with which it lives, let alone the great questions of whether we are going to survive as a human race. Why aren't the churches in the forefront of these discussions? Sometimes I wonder if they aren't full of atheists – people who almost deny that there really is a living God. They seem to be in the business of running some sort of a club.

Strong words, and at times well deserved. But then John Harriott recalled the words of Evelyn Waugh, when asked how he could be a Catholic and yet such an appalling person: 'If I wasn't, I'd be much worse.' Said Harriott:

Human society would be a great deal worse if it were not for the Church, and so would a great many people. I think it is a great mistake to think of the Church as a moral advice bureau, though. I think it undermines people's confidence if churchmen are too assured about what we should do in some particular case. Equally, it undermines them if you begin bobbing and weaving and making all sorts of exceptions.

In short, the Church is just like us: it won't be any better than we – its members or potential members – are. We are not, on the whole, a bad lot. But most of us are rather middle-aged, middle class and tired.

Is Christianity itself worn out? Is religion exhausted? David Jenkins's words ring true to me:

Well, of course Christianity is a myth – I mean, undoubtedly it is a story made up about the universe in response to this mystery . . . The gentleman who thinks that the world will be demystified and that we are problem-solvers, not just in the short and medium term but in the sense of getting all the problems out of the universe, seems to me to believe in a much simpler and much less plausible myth.

And John Bowker added

Religion will never disappear into the sea of its own errors, as Marx and Freud supposed. It will always pick itself up and dust itself down, precisely because of what goes on in the love of God and of one's neighbour as oneself. It's provisional, but it's very well tried. The real point is that religions are corrigible pictures about something that makes its demands upon us, that calls out for explanation.

I emerged from my encounters with the Church and Bible reassured by the uncertainties I had met, and by the honesty with which churchmen had confessed them. It seemed to me the strength of the Bible that people could speak of 'correcting' their religious pictures while preserving their confidence that even those corrections were to be found in it. It seems to me, also, the strength of Jesus that so many of us can find in Him (as I do) a personal image that works alongside us in our daily lives and does not simply rest 'up there' radiating some metaphysical miracle for mankind generally. Jesus' message of inner peace and reconciliation in exchange for spiritual honesty (which I think implies social, political and economic honesty as well) is one that I find totally persuasive. I find the climax of His mission, with its non-violent surrender to a hideous death, moving beyond words; and the effect of His Resurrection (whatever that really was) electrifying. My aphorism 'If Jesus was not God, He is now' is really a form of Bultmann's argument that what matters is not who Jesus *was*, but what He *is* and the demands he forces upon us. But was He God? I come back here to my other aphorism of God saying, in Jesus, 'I am like this. I am so like this that, so far as you can understand, I *am* this.' Yet alongside that I feel I must set Ivor Smith-Cameron's saying:

I don't think Jesus primarily called us to Himself. What He did was to call us together with Him in doing His Father's will. Jesus is the key to our understanding of the nature of God; though God is greater . . . than simply being limited to the person of Christ.

Smith-Cameron was not quite happy with the word 'greater', but I think I understand him, and I agree. Many churchmen would not; but I find they can only explain this in language which for me detracts from the humanity of Jesus, which I find equally important.

I have to say that the doctrine of God revealing Himself to us in loving and meaningful creation, and being revealed through our response to Him in history, does not give me much trouble. Once you trust Him and start looking for signs of Him, it seems obvious. Religion is about response, and the more you give, the more you get back. I found very few churchpeople who doubted that this meant the churches should be involved in political matters, though most of them thought Christians should stand very loosely to party lines and ought not to be afraid of making themselves unpopular with any party or all. Prophecy – speaking forth the truth to society in general – has always been a role of the Church, and I warmed to Father James McShane when he said, 'The ministry of Christ is basically reconciliation, and there are times when we can't afford party politics.'

Out of my inner turmoil, the problem of sin had long haunted me. Sin meant guilt and guilt meant death. When I emerged from that turmoil I was left with the feeling that the Church, and the God it had seemed to present to me, had been radically unfair towards human nature. It was Jack Dominian, Catholic and psychiatrist, who pointed out the positive value of guilt as a warning signal of broken relationship with God or another human being; but he sympathised with my resentment:

The psychological problem in Christianity is that guilt has been related to being completely bad. Your total value disappears. Both Catholic and Protestant traditions have given us this view of man, and it is totally unChristian. You never lose the love of God. Guilt is the warning that temporarily you are out of touch. It should not destroy your essential goodness or separate you from the source of your love.

Together with what I learnt of the Cross as a kind of cosmic pyschotherapy, I think I am now at one with what Christianity has to say about sin. It had appeared to me that the churches taught there was absolutely 'no health in us' and that the only good things about us were on loan from God, by courtesy of His grace. In a sense, all of our lives are on loan to us; but we should not postulate a disapproving, condescending God, rather than a loving Father whose only concern is not that we should be *less* human, but that we should be truly human, willingly choosing His design for us. We come back to love's free will, and to the idea presented to me by John Vernon Taylor, that God's only power is love and that love is vulnerable and suffers.

One of the fascinating things about sin is that in a strange way the Church, like Jesus, is in love with it in spite of itself – though not for itself. For it is ourselves gone wrong, ourselves neglected and distorted, ourselves to be reconciled with God, who is our true selves.

I have suggested that the power of the Cross lies in the fact that it stands at a point where so many different interpretations of the gospel intersect, ranging from the very ancient belief that the God of justice requires a sacrificial payment for sin to the contemporary pacifist view of a non-violent absorption of evil. I do not see why all of these, and more, should not be true simultaneously – though not all of them activate my own conscience. Myself, I am deeply moved now by the realisation that on the Cross we see that God suffers with us the consequences of what we do to ourselves. Christ was made suffering for us, and shows us there is nothing to fear in being vulnerable like Him, for God's love is indestructible: we are constantly forgiven, if only we will reach out and take that forgiveness.

When it came to reconciling this with my own experience of non-Christian religions, two points spoke to me. The first was the Moslem Gai Eaton's contention that 'most people need to believe that their religion is either the only true one or unquestionably the best, if they are to give the whole of themselves to it'. The second, to which Paul Bates led me, was the possibility that 'I am the way . . .' really means 'The way, the truth and the life are all Me – what I stand for'. It is inconceivable to me that a loving creator would have allowed the majority of his children to remain in total spiritual darkness: each group of them has its own way up the mountain, according to where it starts from. It seems to me that each is a valid way over some particular piece of terrain, and that how it tackles that may have something to teach other groups faced with similar problems. In a Western, or westernised, situation I think Christianity (with its Jewish parent) is a better way than any other: it has flexibility, depth, many dimensions and potential for development. And it can reach out in love to other faiths in a way that most of them find it hard to initiate.

The doctrine of the Holy Spirit, of which I made such heavy weather, seems to me essentially about our *response* to God: the divine within responding to the divine without. I am persuaded that it is a useful tool, especially for those seized with the conviction of God's active presence in the Church today. But I have to confess that in spite of this renewal, I am uncomfortable with the doctrine's efforts both to narrow down and define and, simultaneously, to reach out into the deepest mysteries of God.

Much the same thing happened with the Trinity. Again, I can see how the doctrine arose and there is no doubt that many of Christendom's best minds still find it a useful tool. More than that, they find it a convincing expression of the God they experience. I heard many justifications of Trinitarianism, ranging from Professor Bowker's 'two poles of exchange plus the channel of communication between them' through Rabbi Blue's two lovers plus the song to Jack Dominian's mysterious family. All of them seemed to me to be straining our language to the point where the creaking and groaning of it was proving a distraction; and when, in conversation with Rosemary Haughton, we began to wonder 'Why not a Quaternity, to include the feminine element in the Godhead?', I became convinced that it was time to keep mathematics out of religion. So I shall defend Trinitarianism to the death, but I wouldn't want to live there.

Rather to my surprise, I *do* find myself living in the Church, or perhaps in one of its quieter side-chapels. The Church is people, fallible and sinful people, and if it is no better than any other human institution it is certainly no worse. It is nonsense to pretend that we could have our religion without it; and though it has fallen into grave error from time to time, I doubt if it has done as much harm as nationalism, materialism, colonialism, capitalism, communism, fascism, militarism and apathy – with all of which it has been allied at one time or another. You may blame it for compromising or praise it for surviving, according to taste, but at least we have it still, stretching from the urbane to the furious and from the political to the contemplative. It has its howling gaps: it is too tightly bound to its buildings, it is at a loss how to approach the working class, it attracts too few first-rate leaders nowadays. But there are magnificent exceptions to all of these criticisms, and the Church still remains the trustee of much that is finest in our civilisation. Perhaps the worst thing it could do would be to prune its variety artificially, in the hope of impressing the secular world. The world will be more impressed by how Christians live than by how they organise their theology, and that living is up to the laity.

Not that theology is unimportant. As the world becomes more secularised, Christianity becomes increasingly misunderstood by those outside it; and among the things misunderstood are the growing humility, charity and humanity of the churches – a unity of spirit rather than form. I find the women of the churches at the heart of this, and I see in them the Church's great hope.

I would not belittle the worship and services of the Church. They, too, must be of all shapes and styles if they are to reach all conditions of men and women. They are not only the response we owe to God; they are expressions of Christian community, and opportunities for Christian teaching. Above all, they are two-way communication: not merely us throwing words at God, but us listening to what *He* has to say. To me that involves a good deal of silent prayer. But I am aware this does not come easily.

Nor, so far as I am concerned, does the understanding of sacraments. Perhaps the most valuable thing I have learned on this pilgrimage has been that particular language. It is not one I expect to be using frequently myself, but I think I can now understand what others are saying in it, and I find it rich and impressive. Growing numbers in the Protestant churches are finding it meaningful. What that meaning is varies widely and, I think, is bound to: for what is being said is, in effect, beyond words. I rejoice that Christians have found a language that defeats the limitations of words.

The Christian hope – a combination of responsive faith and responsive love – is, in the end, what makes our pilgrimage possible at all. Knowing that God is vulnerable but indestructible, we know that the journey will be strenuous and full of suffering, but that it is not absurd: that it will bring us to the water's edge in the end. It seems to me that I have learnt that the journey itself has its own value, for it shows me that I am not alone and that I cannot expect to leapfrog over the heads of my fellow pilgrims and arrive at the Celestial City by private plane, cleared by the spiritual immigration authorities. Christian faith is the Christian's response to life.

'After this,' says Bunyan,

Mr Ready-to-Halt called for his fellow pilgrims and told them, saying, 'I am sent for, and God shall surely visit you also.' So he desired Mr Valiant to make his will. And because he had nothing to bequeath to them that should survive him but his crutches and his good wishes, therefore thus he said: 'These crutches I bequeath to my son that shall tread in my steps, with an hundred warm wishes that he may prove better than I have been.' Then he thanked Mr Great-Heart for his conduct and kindness, and so addressed himself to his journey. When he came to the brink of the river, he said: 'Now I shall have no more need of these crutches, since yonder are chariots and horses for me to ride on.' The last words he was heard to say were: 'Welcome life!' So he went his way.

Interviewees

Mrs Alison Adcock:
Licensed reader; Church of England

Most Rev. Metropolitan Anthony of Sourozh:
Head of Russian Orthodox Church in Britain

Rev. John Austen:
Advisor for Social Responsibility, Diocese of St Albans; Church of England

Very Rev. Peter Baelz:
Dean of Durham; Church of England

Rev. Roly Bain:
Succentor of Southwark Cathedral; Church of England

Mrs Eleanor Barnes:
Roman Catholic

Kenneth Barnes:
Quaker

Rev. Paul Bates:
Diocesan Director of Training, Winchester; Church of England

Rev. Peter Bide:
Precentor, Christ Church Oxford; Church of England

Rev. Neville Black:
Vicar of Everton; Church of England

Rt Rev. Stuart Blanch:
Archbishop of York; Church of England

Rabbi Lionel Blue:
Leo Baeck College; Reform Synagogues of Great Britain

Rev. Professor John Bowker:
Professor of Religious Studies, Lancaster University; Church of England

Mrs Margaret Bowker:
Reader in History, Lancaster University; Church of England

Very Rev. Tony Bridge:
Dean of Guildford; Church of England

Mrs Elizabeth Broadbent:
Church of England

Rev. Raymond Brown, MA:
Principal of Spurgeon's College; Baptist

Robert Butterworth, SJ:
Lecturer in Theology, Heythrop College, London; Roman Catholic

Rev. Peter Cornwell:
Vicar of St Mary the Virgin, Oxford; Church of England

Rev. Graham Cray:
Vicar of St Michael le Belfrey, York; Church of England

Mrs Mary Cullen:
Member of Scottish Justice and Peace Commission; Roman Catholic

Father Jock Dalrymple:
Priest of St Ninian's, Edinburgh; Roman Catholic

Very Rev. Dean Horace Dammers:
Dean of Bristol; Church of England

Professor Robert Davidson:
Professor of Old Testament Theology, Glasgow University; Church of Scotland

Dr Jack Dominian:
Senior Consultant Psychiatrist, Central Middlesex Hospital; Roman Catholic

C. le G. Eaton:
London Islamic Centre; Moslem

Miss D. R. Etchells:
Principal of Cranmer Hall, Durham; Church of England

Very Rev. Sydney H. Evans:
Dean of Salisbury; Church of England

Mgr Timothy Firth:
Vicar General, Westminster Archdiocese; Roman Catholic

Mrs Valerie Fisher:
Lecturer, Nelson and Colne College; Church of England

Father John Fitzsimmons:
Lecturer in Biblical Theology, St Peter's College, Glasgow; Roman Catholic

Miss Anne Forbes:
Member of Justice and Peace Commission

Rev. Paul D. Fueter:
Consultant for Bible Communication and Distribution for the United Bible Societies; Reform Church of Switzerland

Rev. Frank S. Gibson:
Director of Social Work; Church of Scotland

Dr T. F. Glasson:
Former lecturer, London University; Methodist Minister

Dr Billy Graham:
Evangelist; Baptist

Canon Michael Green:
St Aldate's, Oxford; Church of England

Rabbi Hugo Gryn:
Senior Minister, West London Synagogue

Rt Rev. John Habgood:
Bishop of Durham; Church of England

Professor Charles Handy:
Warden of St George's House, Windsor; Church of England

Rt Rev. Michael Hare Duke:
Bishop of St Andrew's; Episcopalian

John Harriott:
Writer and broadcaster; Roman Catholic

Mrs Rosemary Haughton:
Theologian; Roman Catholic

Very Rev. Eric Heaton:
Dean of Christ Church Oxford; Church of England

Ms Christian Howard:
Member of General Synod; Church of England

Major Norman Howe:
Salvation Army

His Eminence, Basil Hume:
Cardinal Archbishop of Westminster

Canon David Isitt:
Canon, Bristol; Church of England

Canon Eric James:
St Alban's; Church of England

Very Rev. R. C. D. Jasper:
Dean of York; Church of England

Canon David Jenkins:
Leeds University; Church of England

Captain Christine Johnson:
Salvation Army

Very Rev. Dom Edmund Jones, OSB:
Prior of Monastery of Christ our Saviour, Turvey; Roman Catholic

Dr Una Kroll:
Deaconess; Church of England

Professor Hans Küng:
Tübingen University; Roman Catholic

Professor Nicholas Lash:
Norris Hulse Professor of Divinity, Cambridge; Roman Catholic

Major Ken Lawson:
Salvation Army

Dr John Long:
St George's House, Windsor; Methodist

Rt Rev. David R. Lunn:
Bishop of Sheffield; Church of England

Rev. Tim McClure:
Anglican chaplaincy, Manchester Polytechnic

Rev. Steven Mackie:
Practical Theologian, St Andrew's; Church of Scotland

Canon John MacQuarrie:
Lady Margaret Professor of Divinity, Oxford

Father James McShane:
Parish priest, Clydebank; Roman Catholic

Mrs Roz Manktelow:
Winchester; Church of England

Mrs Lorna Marsden:
York; Quaker

Rev. Caryl Micklem:
Oxford; United Reformed Church

Stuart Miller:
Broadcaster, Glasgow; Baptist

Spike Milligan:
Writer and broadcaster; Roman Catholic

Mother Mary Clare, SLG:
Convent of Incarnation, Oxford

Dr Jugen Moltmann:
Professor, Tübingen University

Rt Rev. Lesslie Newbigin:
Selly Oak Colleges, Birmingham; United Reformed Church

Professor Dennis Nineham:
Professor of Theology, Bristol University; Church of England

Rev. Canon Paul Oestreicher:
Canon of Southwark; Church of England

Captain Christine Parkin:
Bedford; Salvation Army

Rt Rev. Lord Ramsey of Canterbury:
Formerly Archbishop of Canterbury

Rev. Donald Reeves:
Rector of St James's, Picadilly; Church of England

Rt Rev. George E. Reindorp:
Bishop of Salisbury (retired); Church of England

Edward Robinson:
Director of Religious Experience Unit, Manchester College Oxford

Rev. Dr Andrew Ross:
New College, Edinburgh; Church of Scotland

Rt Rev. Robert Runcie:
Archbishop of Canterbury

Dame Cicely Saunders, MD:
St Christopher's Hospice, South London; Church of England

Professor Dr Edward Schillebeeckx, OP:
Professor, Nijmegen University

Professor William Shaw:
Professor, St Andrew's University; Church of Scotland

Rev. Canon Ivor Smith-Cameron:
Canon of Southwark; Church of England

Lord Soper:
Kingsway Hall, London; Methodist

Rev. John Stott:
Rector Emeritus, All Souls, Langham Place; Church of England

Rt Rev. John B. Taylor:
Bishop of St Alban's; Church of England

Rt Rev. John V. Taylor:
Bishop of Winchester; Church of England

Rev. Michael Taylor:
Principal, Northern Baptist College

Major Arthur Thompson:
Salvation Army

Dr Denys Turner:
Lecturer in Philosophy, Bristol University; Roman Catholic

Canon William Vanstone:
Chester; Church of England

Rev. David Watson:
Rector of St Michael le Belfrey, York; Church of England

Professor James Whyte:
Professor of Practical Theology and Principal of St Mary's College, St Andrew's University; Church of Scotland

Rev. Maurice Wiles:
Regius Professor of Divinity, Oxford; Church of England

Father Harry Williams:
Community of the Resurrection, Mirfield

Rev. Howard Williams:
Bloomsbury Central Baptist Church

Rev. Dr Rowan Williams:
Church of England

Most Rev. Derek Worlock:
Archbishop of Liverpool; Roman Catholic

Father Timothy Wright, OSB:
Head of Religious Education, Ampleforth College

Select Book List

This is not intended to provide an exhaustive library of the Christian faith. Nor does it include such works as the Authorised Version of the Bible, the Book of Common Prayer, the Oxford and the New International Dictionaries of the Christian Church. I am, however, particularly indebted to the following works and their authors:

John Adair: *The Becoming Church*   SPCK, 1977
Anonymous: *The Cloud of Unknowing and Other Works*   Penguin, 1978
Tony Baker and others: *The Great Acquittal*   Fount, 1980
The Bhagavad Gita   Penguin, 1972
David A. Brown: *A Guide to Religions*   SPCK, 1975
R. E. C. Browne: *The Ministry of the Word*   SCM, 1976
John Bunyan: *The Pilgrim's Progress*   Fount, 1979
Christopher Butler: *The Theology of Vatican II*   DLT, 1981
Patrick Carnegy, ed.: *Christianity Revalued*   Mowbray, 1974
Catholic Truth Society: *The Parish Mass*   1981
Don Cupitt: *The Debate about Christ*   SCM, 1979
            Jesus and the Gospel of God   Lutterworth, 1979
            Taking Leave of God   SCM, 1980
            Who was Jesus   BBC, 1977
Rupert E. Davies: *Methodism*   Epworth, 1976
Doctrine Commission of the Church of England: *Christian Believing*   SPCK, 1976
C. H. Dodd: *The Founder of Christianity*   Fontana, 1974
Susan Dowell and Linda Hurcombe: *Dispossessed Daughters of Eve*   SCM, 1981
Alan Ecclestone: *The Night Sky of the Lord*   DLT, 1980
David L. Edwards: *What Anglicans Believe*   Mowbray, 1974
Charles Elliott and others: *Christian Faith and Political Hopes*   Epworth, 1979
Sinclair B. Ferguson: *The Christian Life*   Hodder & Stoughton, 1981
Michael Green: *I Believe in Satan's Downfall*   Hodder & Stoughton, 1981
Lucas Grollenberg: *Jesus*   SCM, 1978
H. G. Haile: *Luther*   Sheldon, 1981
Richard Harries: *Being a Christian*   Mowbray, 1981
A. E. Harvey: *Companion to the New Testament*   Oxford-Cambridge, 1970
Rosemary Haughton: *The Catholic Thing*   Villa (Dublin), 1979
Peter Hebblethwaite: *The Runaway Church*   Collins, 1975

John Hick ed.: *Christianity and other Religions*   Fount, 1980
Walter J. Hollenweger: *The Pentecostals*   SCM, 1976
Thomas Hywel Hughes: *The Atonement*   George Allen & Unwin, 1949
Martin Israel: *The Pain that Heals*   Hodder & Stoughton, 1981
Paul Johnson: *A History of Christianity*   Penguin, 1976
R. T. Kendall: *Calvin and English Calvinism*   Oxford, 1981
Hans Küng: *The Church Maintained in Truth*   SCM, 1980
                Does God Exist?   Collins, 1980
                On Being a Christian   1977
John Lampen, ed.: *Wait in the Light*   Quaker Home Service, 1981
Nicholas Lash: *Theology on Dover Beach*   DLT, 1979
Ronald Lawler and others, eds.: *The Teaching of Christ*   Veritas (Dublin), 1978
Richard P. McBrien: *Catholicism*   Geoffrey Chapman, 1980
Mother Mary Clare: *Encountering the Depths*   DLT, 1981
James P. Mackey: *Jesus the Man & the Myth*   SCM, 1979
John MacQuarrie: *Christian Hope*   Mowbray, 1981
                Christian Unity and Christian Diversity   Westminster (Philadelphia), 1975
Bill McSweeney: *Roman Catholicism*   Basil Blackwell, 1980
C. F. D. Moule: *The Holy Spirit*   Mowbray, 1979
Stephen Neill: *Anglicanism*   Mowbray, 1978
Edward Norman: *Christianity in the Southern Hemisphere*   Clarendon, 1981
Gerald O'Collins: *Fundamental Theology*   DLT, 1981
Raimundo Pannikar: *The Unknown Christ of Hinduism*   DLT, 1981
Geoffrey Parrinder: *The World's Living Religions*   Pan, 1978
David Perman: *Change and the Churches*   Bodley Head, 1977
Norman Pittenger, ed.: *Christ for Us Today*   SCM, 1968
Karl Rahner: *Our Christian Faith*   Burns & Oates, 1980
Michael Ramsey: *Holy Spirit*   SPCK, 1977
                Jesus and the Living Past   Oxford, 1980
Bruce Reed: *The Dynamics of Religion*   DLT, 1978
Hubert J. Richards: *The First Easter*   Collins Fontana, 1976
John Riches: *Jesus and the Transformation of Judaism*   DLT, 1980
John A. T. Robinson: *Can We Trust the New Testament*   Mowbray, 1977
                Truth is Two-Eyed   SCM, 1979
Edward Schillebeeckx: *Christ – The Christian Experience in the Modern World*   SCM, 1980
                Ministry   SCM, 1981
Ninian Smart: *The Phenomenon of Christianity*   Collins, 1979
D. B. Taylor: *Elements of Christian Belief*   Constable, 1967
Abbé de Tourville: *Letters of Direction*   Amate (Oxford), 1979
W. H. Vanstone: *Love's Endeavour – Love's Expense*   DLT, 1977

Kallistos Ware: *The Orthodox Way*   Mowbray, 1979
E. I. Watkin: *The Church in Council*   DLT, 1960
David Watson: *I Believe in the Church*   Hodder & Stoughton, 1978
Colin Williams: *John Wesley's Theology Today*   Epworth, 1969
H. A. Williams: *Tensions*   Mitchell Beazley, 1976
Herbert Workman: *Persecution in the Early Church*   Oxford, 1980
World Council of Churches: *Sharing in One Hope*   WCC (Geneva),
  1979